*Love* is a Catalyst

# Alana M. Hill

Copyright © 2012 Alana M. Hill

Published by 2Hill Media
a division of 2Hill Consulting Services, LLC
PO Box 2336
Sugar Land, TX 77487
Printed in the United States of America

All rights reserved. No part of this publication may be reproduced, stored in a retrieval system, or transmitted in any form or by any means – for example, electronic, photocopy, and recording – without the prior written permission of the publisher. The only exception is brief quotations in written reviews.

ISBN: 0-9883-2350-8
ISBN-13: 978-0-9883-2350-6

Unless otherwise indicated, Scripture quotations are taken from the *Holy Bible*, New International Version, copyright © 1973, 1978, 1984 by Biblica, Inc.™ Used by permission of Zondervan. All rights reserved worldwide. www.zondervan.com

Cover Design by Expressionistic Designs
Photography by Doss Tidwell

To the loving memory of Louis "Big Pop" Hill, who lost his battle with cancer, but won the hearts of his children.

*Above all else, love each other deeply, because love covers over a multitude of sins!" (1 Pet. 4:8)*

# Contents

Acknowledgements
Foreword

| | |
|---|---|
| 1. A Time to Love | 13 |
| 2. Sizing up Goliath | 21 |
| 3. The Weapons of our Warfare | 29 |
| 4. Fighting with Faith | 41 |
| 5. On the Roller Coaster Ride | 49 |
| 6. The Christmas Miracle | 59 |
| 7. New Year, Same Fight | 69 |
| 8. In the Crockpot | 77 |
| 9. Lord, Help Us All | 83 |
| 10. Are We There Yet? | 95 |
| 11. Staying for the Encore | 103 |
| 12. Analyzing the Results | 111 |
| 13. A Watched Pot Never Boils | 115 |
| 14. Conclusion | 121 |
| Notes from the Author | 127 |

## Acknowledgements

I must start by first giving honor to God, from whom all blessings flow. I want to publicly thank Him for all He has done in my life. He is my redeemer and sustainer, and with him I can do all things. Lord of all I do, I am in awe of His life changing power. His ways are not our ways, and we know that He will use what He needs to use for our good, and His glory!

To my husband, Rodney, who is the most amazing man I've ever known. Your devotion to our boys has been evident every day, and your support of me has been nothing less than spectacular. Thanks for all your input into this project.

To my daddy, Allen Bowers, I express my undying love and gratitude. You have been such a stable constant in my life, and for that I thank you. And watching you transform into Paw-Paw from my wedding day has been so much more spectacular than I imagined. I especially thank you for teaching our boys that DNA does not define family. Love and commitment do.

To my mom, Greta Ann, I give love, honor, respect, and gratitude. You taught me how to fight and how to love (and when to do which). I can't wait to tell your story!

To Pastor Mark Hartman and the Sugar Creek Baptist Church family, I thank you for adopting us into the fellowship and for your constant showing of love.

To Pastor Ralph Douglas West and the entire Brookhollow Baptist Church (The Church Without Walls) family, I extend special thanks. Each sermon and lesson brought me into a closer understanding and relationship with Jesus Christ. It was there that I rededicated my life to Christ and watched my children grow in the Word.

To my extended family (aunts, uncles, and cousins), I thank you for always loving all my boys, proving, like Paw-Paw, that family is more than blood. I thank you for your prayers and covering over my children.

To the soldiers whose faith-walk through this same battlefield encouraged me to listen to God's report, not the enemy's. You have faced this monster, and have the scars to show, I salute you. May you pour courage into all those around you by the telling of your stories.

To my friends, near and far, I thank you for your prayers and support as we endured this trial. Thank you for keeping our arms lifted.

*"When Moses' hands grew tired, they took a stone and put it under him and he sat on it. Aaron and Hur held his hands up—one on one side, one on the other—so that his hands remained steady till sunset. So Joshua overcame the Amalekite army with the sword"* (Exod. 17:12-13).

And to all who encouraged me to share this story, I say thanks and I hope I didn't let you down!

# Foreword

Ten years ago, I met and married Rodney, the man of my dreams, and my best friend. At the moment I became his wife, to my mind I also became another mother to his three boys, Malcolm, Marcus, and Mason. They were eight-, six-, and two-years old respectively when I said "I do, I do, I do, and I do!" It wasn't easy at first, but in time, the younger two slowly accepted the love I offered them, and almost three years later our family welcomed a fourth boy, our baby Matthew. Malcolm, however, was a different story. He pushed us away, his anger blinding him to the love we wanted so badly to give him. He started getting into trouble, dropped out of school, and for a long time, we feared he would never allow himself to be part of our family. He was our Prodigal Son.

They say lightning doesn't strike twice, but I have seen it do just that. For years, cancer was something I read about, something that affected other people. But little by little, that storm moved closer to my home, and to my family. When it first struck, claiming my father-in-law, I sat up and took notice. When it struck a dear friend (whose passion was running marathons), my husband and I began running races to raise money for cancer research. It became a recurrent topic in our family, and it seemed like everywhere we turned, more friends were being diagnosed.

Then, on a sweltering day in August of 2010, lightning struck our home, and our family was changed forever. Receiving the news that our prodigal son had cancer was like being kicked in the stomach. Once the room stopped spinning, I jumped into action. As a mom trying to hold it together, I needed to feel surrounded by family and friends. As the Family Communication Specialist, I needed to share the information via email, knowing in my heart how the story would end. I wanted people to be able to watch God work in real-time. This book is the collection of those messages, entitled Hill Family Update, which told not just Malcolm's story, but how this impacted our entire family.

*"And we rejoice in the hope of the glory of God. Not only so, but we also rejoice in our sufferings, because we know that suffering produces perseverance; perseverance, character; and character, hope. And hope does not disappoint us, because God has poured out his love into our hearts by the Holy Spirit, whom he has given us"* (Rom. 5:2).

## Chapter 1

## A Time to Love

***August 23, 2010: Prayer Request***

Well, I've never been much of a private person, and I've been accused of wearing my heart on my sleeve on more than one occasion, so I can't let this be any different.

A little more than a week ago, Malcolm (our eighteen-year-old prodigal son!) complained of a sore shoulder after dislocating it skateboarding. He also explained to the doctor that his knee had been hurting, so the doctor ordered x-rays. The x-rays revealed a large mass on his knee, so they ordered an MRI. Because of its size and location, he was unable to straighten his leg, and the doctor (an orthopedic specialist) ordered him to use crutches. The doctor had also explained that several things, one of which might be cancer, could cause this mass. We then had to wait three days for the MRI results; meanwhile, Rodney had to leave the country for a class in France.

Wednesday afternoon I checked up on Malcolm, and received a text in reply: "Yep, I have cancer." The MRI revealed that the mass was a 13.7 cm tumor, which almost completely filled the knee cavity (behind the kneecap). That's about the size of a grapefruit! The initial diagnosis was Ewing's sarcoma or osteosarcoma (both are forms of bone cancer, and both are rare). Once we got Rodney back to the States, we then began to jump through the requisite hoops to get Malcolm registered at MD Anderson for further treatment. This meant days of phone calls, and waiting for people to call back. Since we weren't calling about getting our car repaired, but about treatment for our child (who is now an adult), we were anxious and impatient.

Today began the testing at MD Anderson, and more will come Thursday and next week, followed by a prescribed treatment plan. We won't know the doctor's plan for a couple of weeks, but we already know God's plan: "'For I know the plans I have for you,' declares the LORD, 'plans to prosper you and not to harm you, plans to give you hope and a future.'" (Jer. 29:11).

I JUST taught Bible study on this verse the week before

*this happened. He always prepares us!*

*But before you think this is such a sad story, let me back up and tell you how God has already used this.*

*Our oldest had all but given up on school, and on being a part of our blended family. But after getting the first MRI (but before knowing the results), he took and aced the High School Diploma test—not the GED; he is a high school graduate! And he ran into the arms of his dad and me, who had been waiting, and praying, for his return. You see, when the prodigal son returns, the family rejoices!!*

*He had his mom bring him by our house, so I could wrap my arms around him, and visit with him for a while. (Because of the trouble he'd gotten in, I hadn't held him in over a year.) Since my husband was out of town at the time, I was hesitant to let him in at first. Matthew just stared at him as if he were seeing a ghost, and when Malcolm told him, "I'm sorry, little man," I had to leave the room to cry and shout. They hugged, and by the time I returned, Matthew was in his lap, where he loved to be.*

*Malcolm was walking with a limp, and he showed me the huge lump in his leg. It protruded from just above his knee, as if he had a bad frog in his lower thigh muscle. I told him how proud I was about his diploma, and we talked almost as if the past couple of years hadn't happened.*

*When we got confirmation that it was cancer (from his text), all we wanted to do was be together as a family. Malcolm asked to come spend the weekend, and we spent it watching movies and playing Wii, both Hill family favorites!*

*So as you pray, please join our family as we rejoice in the Lord for what he has already done, and what he is about to do! To God be the Glory! I can't wait to hear him share his testimony!*

*God Bless,*

*Alana*

### August 31, 2010: Follow up

*Once again I write this email with mixed feelings. I am still on cloud nine after the Vow Renewal Ceremony we had this weekend to commemorate ten years in our marriage covenant, but we are also in the beginning stages of a tough journey that we can only get through with prayer. This is an emotional roller coaster like no other I've experienced, but I know God is steering the ride!*

*Last Thursday, we spent the entire day at MD Anderson, while Malcolm wheeled himself from floor to floor getting poked, prodded, and scanned. The place was cold, but welcoming. They even had recliners and blankets in the waiting area, with books, puzzles, and computers to help families pass the time. Malcolm remained in good spirits throughout most of the day, flashing his smile, trying to pop wheelies in his borrowed wheelchair, and laughing at the funny content he found on his laptop while we waited.*

*But as the day went on, it all began to take its toll, and he left tired, hurting, and melancholy. The melancholy seemed mostly to result from the medication he had to take* to counter the pain caused by the movements he had to do for the scans. The tumor on his knee was causing him such excruciating agony, he seemed to grimace every time he moved. Since this was his initial workup, they were doing a series of scans and tests. They had to inject him with something to make the images better, and that solution gave him a burning feeling all over—he was not comfortable!

Suddenly his situation seemed so real to me, and I continued to pray for strength, but also rejoicing in the Lord as He brought all Malcolm's parents (mom, dad, and stepmom) to the table together, sharing lunch! By sharing, I truly mean, "You eat this half, and I'll eat the other half." If only kids were pizza, we might not have been so adversarial all these years!

The next day I found myself in the pediatrician's office with Matthew (our youngest), because he had a fever and a sore throat. Fearing having a sick child around Malcolm, I rushed Matthew to the doctor. After he refused to allow them to do a throat swab (screaming, kicking, and biting the stick), I finally broke down in the doctor's office, and the flood gates opened! I cried off and on for the rest of the day...what a release!

Saturday was a day of jubilant celebration. (God is awesome like that!) My beloved and I were celebrating ten years as a couple, and as a family. As we renewed our vows, I couldn't help but reflect on all that God had brought us through! I was speechless at my husband's loving words, and did my best to reciprocate.

*Things were still "brand new" with Malcolm, and it wasn't our weekend, so we were already planning to celebrate with only one of our boys. And with all that has been going on in our lives right now, receiving a call from our minister that he had to leave town for a funeral, and he could not perform the planned ceremony, I should surely have been in the closet holding on for dear life. But I had to hold it together for my family.*

*Looking up some ideas online, my husband and I decided that we would just self-officiate. Then, to our surprise, one of my mom's sisters arrived early to help me set up. Remembering that she was an ordained minister, I asked her to perform the service, and she was honored. Hoping that this could also pave the way to restore our on-again, off-again relationship, I was elated, and the ceremony, which we had in our living room, was beautiful. Rodney's best friend (and best man at our wedding) DJ'd the after-party, and we had a great time.*

*Well, we now have a date for Malcolm's biopsy and he'll be back at MD Anderson this week, Thursday and Friday (the actual procedure is on Friday). We will then get the results of all the testing next week, which will include the treatment plan. I still can't stay sad for long when I think about any of this, because God brought our son back to us, and that's all that really matters. Please join us in praying for strength and peace in the midst of this storm.*

*To God be the Glory!*

*God Bless,*

## A Time To Love

*Alana*

Rodney and I knew when we got married that the odds were against us. We had both just left failed marriages, and he had three young kids. That would be enough to make a lot of marriages fail, but we were determined—some might say stubborn. But because we were such good friends, the rest seemed to fall into place. In a time when marriages are ending in divorce at such a high rate, we were especially grateful to have been sustained by God for ten years!

## Chapter 2

## Sizing up Goliath

*September 8, 2010: The results are in...*

Just as we were beginning to wonder when they would call, the doctor called with the results. It took over a week, and the biopsy confirmed that the tumor is osteosarcoma (one of the bone cancers), although to be honest I don't know if one would be better than the other. What I can say is that God has a plan, and He is working some things out in our lives through this. I even had to ask Malcolm to stop washing dishes. I never thought I'd have a conversation like that! Even with the pain in his leg, he insisted, and I could see that it was his way of saying "I'm sorry."

We went into MD Anderson on Friday morning for an eleven-thirty appointment, but they were able to work him in earlier. As it turned out, the doctor got called into another procedure, so we had to wait for a long time. They had already called Malcolm to the back, and his mom and dad went with him, so I was out in the waiting room by myself. It didn't take long before God sent a couple of women my direction (or me in their direction), and we ended up sharing and praying for what must have been two hours! They were both from out of town, and suddenly I was reminded of how blessed we are to live in Houston, and how God set it up for us to be able to support each other. Rodney came out to check on me, only to realize that I had already made some friends, so he went back to be with Malcolm again.

Here is a description of the biopsy from an eighteen-year-old's perspective:

"They numbed the area with a needle. Then they put some cold gel on my skin, and used one of those things they use on a pregnant woman to see the baby. I asked to sit up so I could see, because it felt like someone was squeezing my leg and it felt weird [that was the biopsy needle]." When the procedure was over, he asked the nurse to give him extra bandages so it would look really serious. Gotta love the gift of laughter! As he began to float in and out of the sedative they gave him, he was telling jokes, then falling asleep, then telling another joke—it really set my heart at ease to see him so comfortable! I nervously watched him eat a snack, worried that his stomach might not be ready, but he was fine.

We spent the weekend with family (first at a reunion, then with close friends). We had no choice but to treat Malcolm like an invalid, because we were outside and it was so hot, but he insisted on going. That was the first Hill family reunion we had all been to together. The rest of the weekend, we just hung out, and enjoyed a "normal" weekend, all the while feeling that it would be the last one for a while. Malcolm asked us what chemo would be like, and all I could say was that it could be like a really bad flu, and that he would feel like crap.

So now with the latest phone call, the doctors know what they are dealing with, and the main doctor said it confirmed his initial plan of three months of chemotherapy, followed by surgery, then more chemotherapy. He mentioned they saw some spots on his lungs (which implies some spreading), so they want to do another scan, but meanwhile, the plan is that Malcolm will meet with the oncologist Monday to schedule his chemo.

So we've got to be prayed up, and buckled up, as it's

*going to be a bumpy ride! I can't thank you enough for taking this journey with us. Each reply and phone call is a reminder that we're not alone. I don't want my son to have cancer, but I know God uses whatever and whomever He needs to use for the good of the Kingdom! I feel like singing a fight song or something, as we prepare for this battle.*

*To God be the glory!*

*God Bless,*
*Alana*

Up until now, our closest family experiences with cancer were at such advanced stages that there was no chemo or treatment of any kind. The most recent, and most painful, of these experiences was with Rodney's dad (Big Pop) just five years earlier. He was diagnosed with advanced stage kidney cancer, and before they could even consider treatment, exploratory surgery revealed it had spread to his bones. He was in agonizing pain, even shouting, "Just kill me now!" from his hospital bed.

He seemed to be taking a turn for the better, so we had agreed that I would proceed with my scheduled business trip to Paris, but while I was there, I got the call that Big Pop had passed. I couldn't get back to my husband fast enough, and I spent the entire flight home kicking myself for leaving in the first place.

We had seen what cancer could do, first to my

grandfather (lung cancer in 2001), and a great-aunt later that same year. It had been creeping closer and closer, and now it had hit us squarely in the heart of our family, and we were terrified, but we had to stand on God's promises, and not let fear consume us.

### *September 18, 2010: Treatments Beginning*

*Well, I don't have nearly as much to say this time, mostly because I'm still processing a LOT of information, most of it not good.*

*Rodney was with Malcolm at MD Anderson today, and they started the day with radioactive isotopes. I was at my desk, frustrated about an email problem, and the boy was getting injected with radioactive materials—really puts a bad Monday in perspective! They needed that for the PET scan (which, I now understand, scans soft tissue). Well, I'll spare you all the terminology (most of which I don't understand anyway,) and I'll fast forward to the meeting with the doctor where he explained that the cancer has metastasized—there is a word I wish I didn't understand! It is really a long word for the "cancer has spread," in this case to his lungs, (a result we were already prepared for to some extent, because my husband won't stay off Google).*

*So, it looks like this Goliath is a little bigger than we'd hoped, but since this didn't catch God by surprise, we know He's already worked it out! If God is for him, who can be against him? When I was eighteen, my biggest decision was* between going to a campus party, or studying, (and at that age I made the wrong choice plenty of times), but here Malcolm is, having to make life-altering decisions about his health...wow! But when the doctor boils it down to him having a bald head for a little while, or the alternative (my fingers can't even type it), then I guess the choice was easy. Malcolm just can't wait to get back on his skateboard!

What won't be easy is getting through these next few months. We now have a calendar of his treatments for the next couple of months, and he goes back to MD Anderson on Friday to allow them to surgically implant a port under his collarbone. This will be used to administer the chemo each time he goes in, and keeps them from having to poke him to draw blood. He will then stay in the hospital, and begin his first chemotherapy treatment Saturday morning. He'll remain there until Tuesday, so he'll essentially spend the weekend in the hospital. This particular chemotherapy "recipe" is administered in two steps, so he'll do step two about two weeks later. Then he'll start the whole thing over again mid-October, which is around the time the doctor expects him to lose his hair. If the tumor responds well, the doctor estimates surgery will be in December. Then, based on the metastatic nature (another big word) of the cancer, they'll do four to six more rounds of chemo in the New Year. That's more than we were expecting, but I guess we just need a bigger stone to knock out this Goliath!!

So much for not having much to say, but you knew I

*was lying. Before I go, I have to share that while at MD Anderson, Malcolm ran into a young lady who had just completed treatments, also for osteosarcoma (this form of cancer is so rare, they were almost the only two there). She had a limp and a long scar on her leg, but she smiled, and told him it would get better! Thank you Lord, for giving him some sunshine!*

*Okay, team. One, two, three...break! Let's get praying, and bombard Heaven with Malcolm's name!*

## Chapter 3

## The Weapons of our Warfare

***September 21, 2010: Ready for Round 1***

Sorry I'm late with this update. It's been a busy, crazy few days. Last week, the enemy tested our faith with facts:

Fact 1: Malcolm has cancer, and it has spread to his lungs.

Fact 2: He is in a lot of pain.

Fact 3: A friend of ours died suddenly on Wednesday.

But FAITH keeps us strong and keeps us going: "I lift up my eyes to the hills—where does my help come from? My help comes from the LORD, the Maker of heaven and earth" (Pss 121:1-2). So as I said last week, this giant is bigger than we'd hoped it would be, but the bigger they are, the harder they fall!

Malcolm went into the hospital Friday to have the port surgically placed under his collarbone for his treatments. That procedure went well, and they later got him settled into his room, complete with a DVD player and a Wii. Although he is eighteen, he is still considered a pediatric oncology patient, so he gets to stay on the "Peds floor." But because he was under anesthesia for the port placement, he didn't get a chance to play with any of his new gadgets. His mom and Rodney were there all day, and I stayed back with the other kids, because I knew they were worried about their brother. As much as I wanted to be at the hospital, the biggest role I knew I could play was to keep communicating, scheduling, and trying to maintain some normalcy for the kids while they're in school. I made the lunch rounds, dropping off Burger King for Marcus (who's a junior in high school), and sitting with Matthew in his cafeteria. As an active member of the PTA there, I spend a lot of time at his elementary school anyway. I couldn't get to Mason, but I'll get over to the middle school next time.

On Saturday, we all visited, and the brothers felt better when they saw Malcolm (and so did I). Walking in and seeing him hooked up to so many tubes was a big shock at first. The kids entered slowly, and were afraid to wake him. The chemo treatment started that morning, and Malcolm got *increasingly tired and nauseated He slept most of our visit, and we let the kids go to the children's center down the hallway. Since there are so many families that come here for treatment, the hospital has a lot of programs and activities for the patients and their families. The next day, Rodney and Marcus went to visit him, and he slept more.*

*His brothers are all handling this in their own way, but they are continuing to pray for their brother. Matthew preached a sermon to me about healing, and Mason was praising in church like I'd never seen before! Marcus is still mostly quiet, and smiles when he hears a good report. He has a worried look permanently etched onto his face, but he keeps just telling me he's okay.*

*Monday, Rodney and I went to visit Malcolm on our lunch break, so that Coach Dad could encourage him to eat. Although Malcolm ate half a sandwich yesterday, he hasn't eaten since, so the doctors are hesitant to release him (he has lost about six pounds already!) Given that he has always been a skinny, small-framed guy, he didn't have six pounds to lose, and you could immediately see it in his face. Since this is a team effort, if you want to help, you can give him one of the pounds that you don't want!*

*We have been working "shifts." His mom has been spending the night; I've been getting the kids around in the red taxi, and Dad is coaching him to stay strong during the day. When Rodney went into Malcolm's room yesterday, the lights were off, and he was just lying there. Coach Dad flipped on the lights, and told him he couldn't fight this* laying down! To that, Malcolm said, "I'm strong. I'm gonna beat this!" Lord, please give him the strength to speak that to himself daily, and for him to be surrounded by cheerleaders! When he comes home from the hospital today, I'm going to greet him with my pom-poms and a few cartwheels! GO TEAM MALCOLM!

Because he is so weak, he needs constant care. So this week, he'll be home (between his mom's house and ours), and because I work from home, he'll spend the days with us. He'll go in again for the next treatment on October 6. He'll be back and forth to MD Anderson for monitoring in between, so please continue to pray for continued strength for him, and his entire team.

God Bless,
Alana

### September 28, 2010: Treatment update

Wow, what an emotional roller coaster. We knew from the moment the doctor said, "Your son has cancer," that this would be a rough road, but sometimes you don't know how rough something will be, until you get into it. Last week had so many dips and turns that I wanted to just close my eyes, scream, and white-knuckle the lap bar (which is what I do on a real roller coaster!) We started the week with a wake for a friend of ours at church. He and Rodney were joking on Facebook one day (Big T was joking that he was *at the hospital with his son, but needing treatment himself). Then the very next day I received word from his wife that he had died suddenly, in the hospital. Their boys were in Cub Scouts with our youngest two, so I was also concerned about Matthew and Mason experiencing loss at this time.*

*A week that went from that grief over a friend, to rejoicing at a child coming home from the hospital and eating, then ending with a frail, sick kid, is not what I call a "good week."*

*Last week, Malcolm completed his first chemo treatment (part one of Round One). It was a true battle for him to stay strong and positive, when all he wanted to do was curl up. When Coach Dad brought him home on Tuesday, he was tired and had no appetite. He was also given seven different medicines to take (mostly to battle the side effects of the chemo). The first thing he asked for was my meatloaf, which I heated up happily, taking seriously my job as team nutritionist. He ate a couple more meals, but then as the week progressed, he ate less and less, and weighed less and less. It was really hard watching him "shrink" in front of us, and his energy level has begun to decrease as well. None of us (Malcolm included) were prepared for him to feel that badly for that long, and by Friday we were all emotionally exhausted. By the time he left our house on Friday, he had lost a noticeable amount of weight, and we could feel his bones.*

*Saturday, Malcolm was still tired, and not eating a whole lot. He weighed himself, and was upset at what the scale said: 110 lbs. Sunday, he was feeling down, but God's timing is amazing, and an extended family gathering at our house, which had been in the works for weeks, went on as planned. Feeling too weak to get out of the car, he had his mom bring him to the curb. When he pulled up, he saw his Paw-Paw, aunts, uncles, and cousins all in seventies' costumes, smiling and happy to see him. That was just the lift his spirits needed. And of special note, they were all "my family," who had considered Malcolm family just as I had, showing him again that family is more than DNA. As his mom gave me the report of what he had eaten earlier that day, I gave him a high five, and did a cartwheel in the front yard (in my Thelma-from-Good-Times get-up)!*

*Monday was his chemo follow-up, and the doctors decided he needed a blood transfusion because his hemoglobin was low. I'll take him tomorrow for that, so please be in prayer for him. We are also trying to make plans for the remainder of Round One, which is scheduled for next week. This poison (I mean drug) is even more potent than the last one, and they are questioning whether he can continue.*

*Wow, what a morbid report. Want some good news? He has been pain-free in his knee since last week, which is great news. The doctor even said the tumor is shrinking! Praise God for healing! And Malcolm ate more today than he did all last week. I just sat there, smiling and watching him eat a bowl of cereal this morning. What a ride we're on! Thanks for riding with us.*

*Oh, and since this is a family update, I would also like to report that all his little brothers proudly brought home great progress reports. Matthew made straight A's! Marcus and Mason each had A's and B's! GO TEAM MALCOLM!*

At this point, we were doing our best to keep things normal for them. We kept the two younger boys in Cub Scouts, even though I seldom had the energy to take them. I was still the president of the elementary PTA, and continued to volunteer as much as I could. That was our normal.

Thankfully, the consulting practice I had started just four years earlier was allowing me the opportunity to set my own schedule, and work from home. This had been vital to our family even without a sick child, but became increasingly important once chemotherapy set in.

### October 4, 2010: Heading to the end of Round One

*Not unlike the previous week, last week proved to have many ups and downs. To recap, the week started with Malcolm barely starting to eat after his last treatment. He weighed in at 110 lbs., had no energy, and the doctors wanted to give him a blood transfusion. That was Monday's report. But as I sat there watching him eat a bowl of cereal on Tuesday, followed by a couple of other meals, I felt I could see the light at the end of the tunnel.*

*Wednesday was an interesting day, and since we are all part of Team Malcolm, it was my turn to venture down to MD Anderson as the coach. I navigated there carefully, like I was carrying precious cargo, and as we got closer, I stopped to get him some breakfast. Thankfully, his appetite was in full swing, and he wanted some French toast sticks from Burger King. I normally don't allow eating in my car, but this was an exception, and I smiled with every bite he took. Funny how perspectives change! I didn't even fuss when he dripped syrup down the front of his shirt!*

*At this point, racing to make the appointment on time (because of the unscheduled but needed Burger King stop), I managed to leave the valet ticket in my car. Being a stickler for time, I was not going to be late, so I let the valet know the issue, and I quickly wheeled Malcolm into the hospital, all the while making silly engine noises. We were like two kids on an adventure. And what an adventure!*

*To summarize the doctor's appointment, his hemoglobin was way up, platelets, too, and he did not need a transfusion after all! This meant our trip to MD Anderson would be cut short for the day. As a matter of fact, his usually dry, matter-of-fact doctor said that the news "made his day." The doctor even said the backache Malcolm was complaining of was probably his body rebuilding bone marrow! After sorting out the scheduling for his next few treatments (complete with his mom on speaker phone), and getting his prescriptions, we headed south toward Sugar Land. I had a hankering for some fried chicken, so I stopped at KFC and we ate on the side of the road. Malcolm devoured his mashed potatoes, and commented on how good they were. So the next time he starts not eating, I'm going to buy a tub of KFC mashed potatoes!*

*That night I filled in my husband on the phone issue. As much as we were trying to work together as a team, leaving past hurt feelings in the past, it was growing increasingly difficult to work with his ex-wife. She was actually debating with the doctor about making appointments that would fit best with her work schedule. Malcolm had to speak up, and remind her that Dad and Lana (that's what they call me) could get him to the appointments. Keeping the animosity-animal at bay, I smiled at his reliance on us, thankful that he could see how much we cared for him.*

*Thursday, he had a quick visit at the Sugar Land MD Anderson location, so that we could use the facility for his next chemo treatments. We had to really push this issue with his doctor, who wanted to personally monitor him, but the trips from our home in Sugar Land to the main campus took more than thirty minutes each way, and the local facility was only ten...and they had free parking! (It cost $15 each time at the main campus.) Given the number of trips we were all making, gas, tolls, and parking fees were quickly becoming a problem.*

*As we were leaving, we ran into a young man a friend had emailed me about. His name is Brent, and he has Ewing's sarcoma. He had offered to call Malcolm to share* some tips with him, but not right away, because Brent was in the middle of his "yucky" week and he wasn't up to chatting much. It was still such a Wow God moment, meeting him there! By this time, Malcolm had begun limiting his contact with his old friends, not wanting them to see him this way.

Then Malcolm had another appointment for blood work on Friday. (Are you getting how time-consuming this all is? It's necessary too, of course.) Thankfully, his high-school friend was off that day, so he took Malcolm to his appointment, and they hung out for a while.

Anyway, God smiled upon all of us over the weekend with the gorgeous weather, and we enjoyed a family day out on Saturday, complete with movies and burgers for everyone. When we got home, Malcolm commented that his hair had been falling out, and he wanted his dad to cut it off, so we of course turned that into a family project as well, with Coach Dad on the clippers, and me on the towel to exfoliate and smooth his now bare scalp. Marcus provided moral support, and vacuumed up the hair from the floor. There he sat...bald...and it was once again so real to us all! Given that Rodney has started shaving his head after we started dating, we were used to a bald Hill, but now there were two.

The next day, we all went to church together, and it was Malcolm's first time back there in over a year. No one in church had seen us all together in a long time, and we relished the attention that it brought. A family friend was *singing in the choir, and after service told me she couldn't stop crying when she looked in our direction, and saw us all sitting there together. I had made no secret about how badly I wanted all my family together. I was filled with joy seeing Malcolm at church with his knit cap on, and weighing 124 lbs.! Glory to God!*

*This week will be tough. He has an infusion of chemo on Tuesday, followed by some "rescue" drugs. The more I learn about chemo, the more it scares me. It seems like you have to choose the lesser of two evils, and we're constantly worried about the long-term liver and kidney damage chemo can cause. They are doing his chemo outpatient now, so he'll be at his mom's this week. Then, after a couple of days, he'll do it again, likely at our house. There is no special cancer-care-custody agreement, so we're making it up as we go. Thanks for your prayers! He'll have a week off, and then start the whole thing over again (beginning with the treatment from two weeks ago).*

*Oh, I'm sorry! Did you want the short version? Malcolm is eating, and even hung out with his friends this week. He doesn't need a blood transfusion. Next chemo treatment is Tuesday, and he is losing his hair. Why didn't I just say that? It wouldn't capture the essence of the journey! Thanks again for riding and praying!*

*God Bless,*
*Alana*

My inbox was once again flooded with supportive responses. To think that people cared enough to stop what they were doing when they received an email about our family was very encouraging. Usually people asked what they could do to help. Others offered words of encouragement and prayers.

Unfortunately, though, they weren't all encouraging (you can't win 'em all). A friend told me on the phone that she couldn't read my emails, that they were too depressing. I thought to myself, "I'm sorry. I'll try to make my son's cancer a little less hard for you," and I deleted her from my list. I hated that she will miss out on what God is getting ready to do, but I needed to stay surrounded by positivity, and some things you just don't say.

Sending the email also became a way of me not having to hear the obituaries that tend to come when you tell someone a loved one has cancer. We knew all too well the statistics and possibilities, but it was still surprising that so many people's first reaction was to tell me about their friend/cousin/mom/dad who had died a horrible death from cancer. I understand they were trying to relate, but that was fear talk, and we just didn't allow it in our spirits.

# Chapter 4

## Fighting with Faith

***October 11, 2010: Finishing up Part Two of Round One***

I know I've claimed it before, but I mean it this time: I will be brief, partly because I'm tired from the flu mist we all took for the team, and partly because this past week is pretty easy to summarize.

Malcolm handled yesterday's treatment like a champ, and after a good nap, he was ready to eat! Way to go, Mal! We also found out that there will be a benefit walk/run for Brent, and we plan to participate and show our support.

## Love is a Catalyst

*Brent and his wife have been very supportive of all of us!*

*The week started off with some testing to confirm that Malcolm was ready to take the infusion of high-dose methotrexate (something Malcolm can say very clearly!) The doctor gave the go-ahead, and Coach Papi Nino arrived to take Malcolm for his infusion on Tuesday. Papi Nino is Malcolm's grandfather on his mother's side, and he and his wife came into town from San Antonio to help out. Malcolm slept through most of the treatment, basically sitting in a chair with a slow drip. Once that was over, he had to be monitored a bit, and he made it home by the middle of the day. He ate, and then slept for the rest of the day. He was sent home with a backpack pump to give him the hydration fluids to help flush the drug out of his system.*

*Wednesday was a nice high on the roller coaster ride (in many ways). A friend met me for lunch and brought a care package for Malcolm. After lunch was over, I called to make sure Mal was awake, so I could deliver the package. He said he was sleeping, but that he wanted to see me, and he wanted to show me his new room. He sounded giddy, so I ran straight to see him with the box in hand, ready to surprise him, and glad he was up. You see, the friend I had dined with forwarded one of my emails to a friend whose son just happens to be a professional skateboarder. God is so amazing like that! The box contained brand-new shoes, t-shirts, and jeans from a popular skateboard company. When I showed Malcolm what was in the box, he smiled from ear to ear, and couldn't wait to call a friend of his who used to* skateboard with him.

I wanted to jump out of my skin, I was so happy watching him feel so elated. To add to it, Malcolm was prescribed some pills to help with his appetite, and they were working so well that he was inhaling a chili cheese dog as we were talking. So not only did he get something he really wanted, but he gave me something I really wanted—to see him eating and smiling! So big ups to Toni and Renee. Thanks for letting God use you!

Unfortunately, the rest of the week wasn't as joyful. Malcolm didn't want the side effects of the appetite pill (it contains marijuana, so he was high!), so his appetite declined after that. By Thursday evening, he was fatigued, and had chills. Worse, he began to get more mouth sores, one of the many known side effects of the chemo drug he was taking. So from Friday onwards, he rested, and barely ate. At least, because he had spent a couple of days consuming everything he could get his hands on (he had the "munchies"), his weight remained normal! While he rested, Rodney, Matthew and I headed for some roller-coaster fun in San Antonio, preparing for the next game!

Coach Dad was in the game this week, and took Malcolm to his doctor's appointment. The doctor was pleased with Malcolm's progress, and gave him something to help with the mouth sore pain (which he described to me as pretty severe). Even better, to keep him from getting more mouth sores, the doctor made this a BYE week! No infusion this week. We all get to take the week off! Hallelujah. So the schedule has been updated, and this round will finish next week (with a repeat of last week), and his next round will start right after that. His surgery will likely be the second week of December, just in time to get home for Christmas!

Thanks again for "tuning in."

God Bless,

Alana

For a while, he had been smoking in his room in his mom's house. The walls, his bed, and even the baseboards reeked of it. When he had started getting in trouble with the law and skipping school, she took his door off and took the frame and everything off his bed. She tried to administer tough love, but Malcolm had completely ruined the place (even the hall leading to his room). His room looked like a crack house, and I would have emotional setbacks when I'd visit him, flashing back to my childhood.

### October 19, 2010: First BYE Week

Last week was a bye week, which in football means no game, and in cancer treatments means no visits to the doctor (except the one on Monday that determined the doctor would give him the week off). A week off? Hmm, well, Malcolm could take a week off from treatments, but not a week off from cancer. At first, I sort of took it that way, as if we could almost forget for a few days...not so! Like I told Mal when he got the diagnosis, the cancer is in his legs (and lungs), but it's also in our lives, and we are all dealing with this together in our own ways.

For me, that meant organizing things (like the proverbial Team Mom), and trying to take care of the home front, while others on the team get Malcolm to his treatments. That's when I took on the role of Communications Specialist, because someone had to capture this story. Coach Dad researched the footage, and prepared the strategy to defeat the "enemy," all the while concerned that the cancer could come back. But since that was only part of his job, he also had to hold it down at work.

Little brothers try to continue to be normal. Marcus has a job, and is now getting ready to get his license. Mason is transitioning into middle school and even has his eye on a couple of co-eds (and still fighting with his little brother over who is the baby of the family). Matthew is, well, let's just say he is even more intense than before (more highs and lows). Basketball season will be starting for him soon, and that will be a welcome distraction for us all.

Malcolm went to Matthew's basketball evaluations, and got to see him play for the first time (remember, the prodigal missed quite a few family moments). Now all the boys are looking forward to cheering Matthew on this season!

So, as much as I would have liked for a bye week to mean goodbye cancer, it only gave us (me) more time to reflect, and in turn, to become more melancholy. As the shock wears off, the calls become fewer, and the loneliness sets in. I love that I have a large family, but that means a lot of people to be there for, so I have to be careful and take care of me! At times like this, I really miss my mom!

Thanks for listening. Oh, and I hope to see you at the Brent Event this coming Saturday.

*God Bless,*

*Alana*

We were all gearing up to show our support for Brent by participating in a walk (they also had a 5k run). Malcolm told me how badly he wanted to run in the race, and given that he completed a 10k with us before with almost no training, it would have been possible previously.

The event was early in the morning, and we knew Malcolm needed his rest, so we just called him from the park. Matthew ran the family mile in his brother's honor, along with some cousins who had joined us in support. The entire function reminded us that good can always come from a bad situation.

### October 24, 2010: End of Round One

*Okay, Round One is officially over! Goliath is still there looking at us, but he's getting smaller! This thing is going down! Malcolm 1, Cancer 0. GO TEAM MALCOLM!*

*Last week was the last infusion from Round One, and we've all got this down pat now. On Monday, Mal went in for his treatment. They put some medicine in an IV that he carries in a backpack, and he had to go in every day at the same time to get the bag changed (and to change the battery on the pump). Because he was having mouth sores, the doctor postponed the last of the Round One treatments to last week. This was the same chemo drug he took two weeks ago, but this time he didn't experience any mouth sores, and hardly any nausea. Praise God! He ate like a....well, like a teenager, wanting chili-cheese anything.*

*The highlight of the week for all of us was celebrating Marcus getting his driver's license, AND starting his first job at a nearby grocery store. Our baby is growing up! The high point for me was watching Malcolm devour the homemade chicken noodle soup I made for him. He kept talking about how much he wanted some, and I happened to find the ingredients in the refrigerator and the store (that's what I told him anyway)—a dab of this, and touch of that, and a little sprinkle of love, and voila! Funny thing is I'd never made it before, but I thought, "How hard could it be? I AM an engineer."*

*Mal was too tired to go to the Brent Event on Saturday morning, but both Brent and his wife asked about him, which was amazing because Brent is having surgery on his lungs Monday. (Remember, Brent is the guy with a similar bone cancer who lives here in Sugar Land.) Matthew ran the mile with a few of his cousins, and I was forced to run with them. It was supposed to be a one-mile walk, and although we had run two half marathons a while ago, we weren't really in race shape.*

*By the afternoon, Malcolm thankfully felt well enough*

to go to the movies—and he was even more excited that his friend bought his ticket, and his newly-employed younger brother bought him a hot dog! He has signed up with the Make a Wish Foundation, and has asked for a PlayStation3 or flat screen television. Not too much to ask! When he showed me his application a few weeks ago, we talked about "life threatening" versus "terminal," and he seemed to feel encouraged to stay the course with his treatments. After completing a round, though, he is beginning to get weary.

So this week we start Round Two. He has several appointments scheduled for Monday at MD Anderson, and depending on how the test results look, he may get his infusion of the first drug he had. That one was a doozy; it made him extremely nauseated and tired. Heck, the nurses called it the "Red Devil"! He is actually hoping for another week off, but that would mean the hospital would have to postpone the surgery. We're praying he can keep his fighting spirit going, but he's afraid after the last reaction he had. I'm just gonna keep my pom-poms going, and keep cheering for the team. Let me hear you!

Thanks for prayin' and cheerin'!

God Bless,
Alana

## Chapter 5

## On the Roller Coaster Ride

***November 4, 2010: Starting Round Two***

*OK, I'm not sure how I got so far behind. It could be the fact that my PC was at the doctor's over the weekend, or it could be all the acting out behaviors we dealt with around here (notice I say dealt with – past tense!)*

*So, last week was interesting. We took Malcolm to the doctor on Monday to start round two of his chemo, but he was nervous about starting it, and wanted to give himself another week. . Our first reaction was to cheer him through it to keep his spirits up and to remind him to stay in the fight, but ultimately it was his decision (he is 18!), the doctor was on our side at first (praising how well he had been bouncing back), but then he stepped out and came in with a different tune. . He measured the tumor and noted that it had grown! It was very sobering to hear the doctor talking about continuing the course to improve his survival rate...did he say "survival"...the engineer in me came out and I started re-analyzing the problem, sure that we had to do something. . Here I was trying to get him back on his skateboard, and the doc is trying to keep him alive...wow!*

*Coach Dad and I spent the next couple of days reflecting on the doctor's visit, and replaying a lot of his words in our heads...I say our, because we rolled over a couple of nights to find that we were both awake thinking the same thing...Mal took the week off, but the cancer didn't. We were officially scared.*

*He had an MRI done that Thursday to take a look at the bone tumor. But other than that, he had a "week off".*

*I won't get off topic by telling you about the wonderful girlie day and sleep-over I had Friday with my bestie, complete with matching PJ's from Pink and new lip-gloss from MAC...because that would be irrelevant...almost, if it weren't for the fact that as a caregiver I have learned that I MUST take time for myself.*

*Once the concern of him taking another bye week passed, we just enjoyed each other and his sense of humor. After all, he was going to have to get treated again the next* week, so when Monday came around this time, he was ready!! He took the treatment like a champ and it hasn't been nearly as bad as he thought it would be. He's been up and about, eating, and in really good spirits! And the doctor said the tumor appears to be making bone, which is apparently good news. Praise God for his awesome wonders!

He'll have next week off, then the last 2 infusions of this round (which are spread out), then surgery looks like the week before Christmas. Of course, I'll keep you posted (seeing as I'm the communications specialist and all).

Thanks again for praying and cheering. He is getting spoiled with the care packages, but please, keep them coming! He is a huge movie buff, so he would welcome any Blockbuster gifts cards or the like. He's got a lot of time on his hands, and will have more after the surgery as it will be harder for him to get around.

God Bless,<br>Alana

### November 11, 2010: Round Two is Not Going So Well

Well, I had this nice upbeat update to send, and then today happened. But let me start from last week. Malcolm started Round two of his chemo on the same drugs he started with last time. As I mentioned before, the infusions went well, and he was not as sick as the last time. The infusions were over three days, then they gave him IV hydration, so he had his "backpack" until Friday. He had what would have just been a ho-hum weekend, but he got a <u>surprise visit</u> from the professional skateboarder that sent him the gear, Darrell Stanton! He was still giddy when he was telling me about it hours later. And amazingly, he just kept calling him "tall"...

Malcolm didn't have any appointments this week other than routine blood work to ensure all was going well, so for the most part, he could just chill. Tuesday I went to check on him and to get the boys for church, but he was curled up on the sofa looking exhausted. He said he didn't feel well, but that was to be expected. He was too tired to visit, let alone go to church. As time went on, he got sicker, and he mentioned last night that he thought he might have a fever. A sty developed in his eye, making it look a little swollen, and his throat and nose were all hurting. Coach Dad called to check on him, and Mal asked him if he'd come to the doctor with him.

When he went in for his blood check today, they took his vitals. He had a temperature of 99, so they told him to go home and rest and drink lots of fluids. I took his temp later and it went to 101. When I rechecked and it was 100, it meant it was time to head to the hospital according to the chemo orders. Just as we were trying to figure out where to *go, the doctor's office called, and said that his blood work showed a low blood counts and that he'd need to go to the ER.*

*Malcolm received calls from three different nurses, and after some conflicting information and a "who's on first" scenario, Coach Dad took him to the hospital. They waited the remainder of the afternoon to be admitted, and as of my typing this email, Malcolm is just getting settled into his hospital room. They are planning to keep him at least three days. They put him on IV antibiotics, so he was starting to feel a little better, but he'll likely get a blood infusion tomorrow.*

*So please keep those prayers coming. I feel like we're taking a knee in the middle of the first quarter while a man is down on the field – we need you back in the game to win this thing! You know I love football! Let's go Malcolm...let's go!*

*God Bless,<br>Alana*

### November 30, 2010: Round Two, and Thanksgiving

*Now that the sugar binge of Thanksgiving is over, we are now back to reality. Since we had some time off (no work and no chemo), we thought it would be nice to take a trip. We decided on a quick getaway to Florida to visit family for the holiday, and to take the youngest Hill boy to*

*Disney World (his brothers have already been).*

*Our escape to the "Happiest Place on Earth" sure came at a good time. After coming down with some sort of bug, Malcolm spiked a fever and got very weak. As a chemo patient, we had to rush him to the emergency room so they could monitor him. They ended up admitting him for a couple of days, and kept him on IV antibiotics. Amazingly, while visiting him, we bumped into a good friend in the elevator who was there for his own follow-up treatment. This cancer monster is everywhere! Malcolm got out of the hospital on Saturday, November 13. I was the next to get sick, complete with throwing up and chills. Finishing up that last week at work and school proved to be a challenge as well, and halfway through it, Marcus got sick, too.*

*It wasn't our year to have them for Thanksgiving, so the boys came over the weekend before, and we enjoyed our own early holiday including a visit to Granny Mary's (Rodney's mom) that Saturday. She hadn't had a chance to see Malcolm since he got sick, and she was happy to be able to rub his bald head.*

*We enjoyed Sunday worship service together (all six of us), sitting in the pew with our little ducks in descending height order. I was reminded again how God restored our family, as the guest preacher quoted the twenty-third Psalm on our church's twenty-third anniversary: "...he restoreth my soul...for his name's sake..." (Pss. 23:3, KJV) God restores us to where we should be, who we should be, and what we should be because HIS name is on the line! At*

Malcolm's request, I made meatloaf, and I happily watched them all devour it, especially since we wouldn't be together for Thanksgiving.

Then Coach Dad, Matthew and I boarded a flight to Tampa, drove to Orlando for a four-day visit, then back to Tampa and the flight home. The highlight of the trip (aside from the Hulk ride at Universal Studios) was watching Matthew copy his older cousin as they both walked around the house in basketball shorts with no shirts on. It was funny watching both little basketball phenoms, seeing how much alike their bodies were, and how similar their personalities were, (both being the babies of their bunch).

It was especially nice seeing Matthew so carefree in the midst of this storm—that is, until we went to Disney World. The park was only mildly received by the little seven-going-on-seventeen-year-old who just wanted to ride coasters, and was very agitated by the lines. He was reminded of his age by losing two baby teeth on the trip, although he said the money didn't come from the tooth fairy. It must, he said, have been from me or God! Where does he get this stuff? While we were gone, we talked to the boys daily, and Rodney and Malcolm texted constantly...pretty cool!

So now we're back in Houston, and Malcolm has started the second treatment in Round Two, and he seems to be doing well so far. He was sick and pukey yesterday, but he was feeling a little better today, and hopefully he'll feel even better tomorrow. His doctor said he is responding well, *and the lung tumors have not grown, which is good news. We'll find out Monday what day they are going to do the knee surgery, to remove the primary tumor and reconstruct his knee. Malcolm will need to be in the hospital for a week, and they are trying to do all that before Christmas. His hair is all gone, and his eyebrows are on their way out.*

*After the new year, we'll find out when they want to do surgery on his lungs to remove the tumors they found there, but for now, we're just planning to enjoy Christmas, because this will be our first one all together in a while...God ROCKS!!*

*Now, back to working off this turkey and trimmings. Have a great week, and thanks for praying.*

*God Bless,*

*Alana*

There was an unfortunate lowlight of the trip. We were staying with my aunt (my mother's sister), and we felt she could use the company, given how sad she had been sounding on the phone. We had only recently begun speaking again after an almost two-year estrangement, and it was clear that we needed each other, talking on the phone almost daily at this point.

Both the stress of the holidays, and her recent college send off for her baby girl, seemed to make her depressed. As I watched my aunt walk around in obvious pain, I had flashbacks to my mother's own coping (their resemblance is uncanny), and I found myself in my husband's arms, sobbing for comfort. With all that we had going on in our lives, all I could keep saying was how much I wanted to help my aunt, because I hadn't been able to do the same for my mom when she needed it. I felt just as helpless as I had when I was a teenager watching my mom battle her demons. Needing all my strength to care for my family in this crisis, I tried to just remove the images from my mind, and began praying for God to heal her heart.

I had also resumed writing my memoir, which had been a labor of love for years, finally speaking publicly about the pain I endured as a result of my mother's drug addiction and murder when I was a teen. That writing was very cathartic as I didn't want to carry any of the pain from my past while fighting for our son's life, but at the same time it required me to relive a lot of pain.

## Chapter 6

## The Christmas Miracle

***December 7, 2010: We decked the halls***

Well, as usual, this past week has been bittersweet. Last week, Malcolm finished the second treatment in Round Two of his chemo, complete with the backpack, and daily trips for blood work. Yay Team Malcolm! He didn't have much of an appetite, but he wasn't quite as nauseated as last time, so that was good. He did, however, have some mouth sores that kept him from eating, and made him really uncomfortable. He is completely bald now, and his facial hair is gone. His eyebrows are very thin, and from some angles appear to be missing. But he has been the most loving and considerate person, being sure to not "inconvenience" anyone (despite my telling him constantly that this is OUR fight!)

Over the weekend, we enjoyed our Friday movie and pizza night (the only Hill family tradition we've been able to do consistently for ten years). Saturday we all seemed to scatter: Marcus had to work all day; I had a ministry meeting; and the rest stayed home, and watched movies. Malcolm hadn't eaten all day, because he was waiting for me to make him some soup (with my special touch, he said). I hated that he was waiting for me, but I loved that he needed me, and even more so, that he wasn't afraid to say it. We've come so far in our relationship, not really talking about the past, but being extra kind to build a sweet future.

Sunday, we took the Hill family Christmas picture in one take—a new family record. We didn't do one last year, because Malcolm's absence was too painful. We actually took a "serious," and a "silly" pose. In both shots, I sat between the two bald guys, and even gave Mal rabbit ears. Then, after high-fiving ourselves for a successful photo shoot, we decked the halls, complete with corny versions of the Twelve Days of Christmas.

My highlight? It was Malcolm saying out of nowhere, "Lana, I love you." I almost dropped the Christmas ornament I was fumbling with! I didn't get to baby him as an infant, but I've been given a chance to do that now, and he is so aware of how much he is loved! We know that our kids will leave the nest, and we are preparing them daily for that journey, but I never want them to just fall out of the nest, and not look up.

Monday was sobering. The surgeon has scheduled his knee surgery for next Thursday, December 16. It will be a six- to eight-hour surgery, and I'm trying to figure out when the surgeons use the restroom. The doctor seemed confident that the limb-salvage procedure will be successful (in other words, no amputation), but Malcolm asked him lots of questions, and expressed his concern about waking up sans a leg. He was pretty clear that if there was a chance that he might eventually lose his leg, then the doctor might as well just plan to take the leg now. This was just Malcolm's way of trying to maintain some control, which I understand. After his surgery, he'll be in the hospital for up to five days while the incision heals. But praise God, he'll be home for Christmas!

For those curious about details, the surgeons are going to remove about half his femur (thigh bone) and kneecap, and replace them with metal, then use some special synthetics to replace his cartilage. They will use cement to bond the metal to the bone to keep it all in place. He will be the Six-Million Dollar Man when this is over, and he is eager to get running again.

The doctor wasn't too optimistic about the running, explaining you can't jump on these metal things, but Mal didn't let them stop him in the conversation. *"I WILL run again," he told the doctor! With God, all things are possible!*

*To God be the glory!*

*God Bless,*<br>*Alana*

I hadn't heard Malcolm tell me he loved me (or anyone in our family) for so long, I was speechless. The vulnerability his illness created began to knock down walls that he had erected these past few years. We have always been a huggy-kissy family, greeting with a "hello kiss", and departing with a "good-bye kiss", but his sudden departure made that impossible to do with him.

When Matthew arrived home safely from the NICU, my husband and I were so united by the experience, we proudly proclaimed that there was nothing that God could not do! I was now the happy mom of four boys. I had told my three older boys from the beginning that I loved them like they were my own, always referring to them as my boys or my sons (I only used "step-" with the doctor), but once I held my "own" in my arms, I found I could say it without any doubt: I had four sons. We encouraged (actually insisted) that our three older boys never refer to Matthew as their half-brother, not wanting to have any distance in their relationship. I finally had the family I had prayed and waited for…or so I thought.

## December 17, 2010: Surgery was a success

*I have not been able to sit still long enough to think, let alone write an update. This is such a wonderful time of year, but such a BUSY time!*

*Last week, Malcolm was invited to attend the Lombardi awards. Through a foundation that works with MD Anderson, he was given a tuxedo rental, a limo ride, and a ticket to the event, which was held at the George R. Brown Convention Center in downtown Houston.*

*In typical Team Malcolm fashion, this was not a smooth day. Our beloved boy waited until the day before the event to decide that he wanted to go. He kept protesting the idea, saying he didn't want to be someone's charity case. This late play meant his mom had to rush him to a tuxedo fitting, and then rush him to MD Anderson to catch the limo. Unfortunately, she got a flat tire on the way to the limo pickup point, so Coach Dad had to run to the rescue to pick up the tuxedoed kid, and drop him off at the event. He was able to ride home in the limo, and he called his friends to tell them about this cool experience. Funny, we recall him not wanting to go...*

*So on to the surgery. Oh but first, a quick mention that Matt had his first basketball game of the season, and he scored twenty-two points! We recorded the game, and watched it as a family on Tuesday night, with Matt's biggest fans (Malcolm, Marcus, and Mason) commenting on each play!*

*So Thursday came, surgery day, and we arrived at the hospital at nine-thirty. Mal was barely awake, but he was ready to get this done. The night before, he and I agreed to call him The Bionic Man when it was over! Malcolm had to sit around and wait in pre-op for about two hours, and we rotated going back to see him, two at a time. Meanwhile, the kids were in school, trying to concentrate on finals, but all the while worried their brother might wake up without his leg. They asked lots of questions leading up to this day, most concerning his ability to walk afterwards, even worrying that he could die in surgery.*

*We sat in the waiting room, and finally got an update at two that surgery had started at twelve-thirty. Then we got another update at four that surgery was still going on, but that they were still waiting on pathology to confirm that the leg was okay. All the while, a good friend of mine had camped out in the waiting room with us.*

*Then at about six, the doctor came out and gave us the full story. The surgery went well, and Malcolm's leg is clear of cancer! The doctors replaced half his femur and his knee, and with some serious physical rehab, he should resume full use of his leg, which according to the doctor means walking, but we know Mal's plan! Yay God! Whoop! Hallelujah! (Hey, I'm a Christian Texas Aggie!) He'll be in the hospital for at least a week. We're all still hoping and praying Malcolm will home for Christmas, but if not, we'll bring Christmas to his hospital room!*

*Next up, beating the hell outta the cancer in his lungs!*

*He'll resume chemo for a few months, and have lung surgery sometime within that period. Of course, I'll let you know when I know!*

*Thanks for praying and cheering!*
*To God be the glory!*

God Bless,<br>Alana

All along I was using these emails to communicate both feelings and information. I had leaders from our church on the email list, and I wanted them to be aware that Malcolm would be hospitalized close to Christmas, and that he ran the risk of losing his leg.

For all the fun we were having, trying to enjoy the holidays, we were terrified of the upcoming surgery. That was the first thing Malcolm noticed about Brent when we met him in person—Brent's missing leg. We locked eyes and noticed the same thing, praying then that it would not also be Malcolm's fate.

### December 31, 2010: The year is almost over

*As this past year comes to close, I can't help but pause and reflect. It took until three in the morning for him to get to his room, and he had a really rough night, complete with a rookie nurse who may need to make a career change. The* next morning, though, he was all smiles, happy to have his leg, and eager to get on with fighting the cancer in his lungs. He began physical therapy right away, and took his first steps on Saturday (just two days after his surgery) in front of cheering little cousins and brothers who had come to visit him, and encourage him. And of course, I took pictures and video and tried not to cry...unsuccessfully! It was even better than watching a baby take his first steps, because in your mind, a baby is just doing what he is supposed to do. But for this victory, the odds were against him, and just having the leg was such an incredible blessing.

After biting our nails, and praying that he would be home for Christmas, his leg began to swell. He refused to eat the hospital food, and it was the responsibility of whoever was visiting him to get him pizza, burgers, or whatever else he decided he wanted. Knowing that no one wanted to see him not eat, he had twenty-four-hour room service by non-hospital personnel. He became more and more agitated by the fact that he was still in the hospital, and his teenage rebellion began to kick in.

He was eventually discharged on Thursday, December 23, just two days before Christmas! We were eagerly awaiting his return, and since his mom was at the hospital, she was bringing him to our house. Not having to drive, I began pulling out streamers and noisemakers to welcome him home! But as soon as he got in, he went to the movies with a friend; despite our protests...he is eighteen after all. We understood his desire for freedom after being trapped in *the hospital but we were also looking forward to just spending some time together. More importantly, we didn't think he was physically ready to walk around a movie theater, but he was being stubborn. He confided the next day that he shouldn't have gone (after waking up in agony), and he slowed down after that.*

*We celebrated with tons of family the next day on Christmas Eve. Knowing that Malcolm wouldn't be mobile after his surgery, we had made plans to have my mom's side of the family come over.*

*I can't stop shouting about how good God is, to bring my family back together! It was for Him to decide how and when, and we don't doubt Him for a second. To think, we found out our oldest son had cancer just a couple of days before celebrating our tenth wedding anniversary, and ten years as a family. We knew then that God would sustain us, and He has sent many of His angels to help us in this struggle. This battle is still far from over (we're not even halfway through the doctor's treatment plan), but we can look ahead, and know this battle is already won!*

*So the New Year will start with a new chemo drug (starting January 10) for a week. But for now, we are celebrating the victory over the tumor in his leg!*

*To God be the glory!*

*God Bless,*<br>*Alana*

## Chapter 7

# New Year, Same Fight

*January 15, 2011: The New Year has begun*

Well, I must say, this is the most heavy-hearted I have been since this whole journey began. We are all now pretty weary from these past few months: the trips to the doctor, the constant shuffle of kids and work, the refusal of our "patient" to follow the instructions of his parents or his doctors, and the energy to keep everyone involved.

At the beginning of a race, runners familiarize themselves with the course to know where the hills and turns are, knowing that it will help them plan their pace and *strategy. The unprepared runner doesn't know what is around the next turn, and may sprint too soon and hit a wall in the race. The outcome of the race is also determined by the will of the runner, and our runner doesn't have his head in this race. Malcolm doesn't want to train or eat right. The metaphors are all nice, except this runner is my son, and he refuses to do what he needs to do to stay alive. His coaching staff and cheerleaders can't convince him. And it is becoming unbearable to watch! I pray daily for patience to deal with this patient, and the strength to carry on. I pray that he will surrender himself fully to the Lord who is his sustainer. Thankfully, we serve a God who answers prayers, but the waiting never gets easier.*

*Now that the tumor has been removed from his leg, we need Malcolm to stay focused on the real threat, which is the cancer in his lungs! I have met people with no leg before, but never someone with no lungs! Still, since he wants a good quality of life (and we all want that for him), he will need to put in the effort to rehab his leg, which so far he has not done! That now comes in combination with longer chemo treatments, now scheduled for eight more months, because the cancer in his lungs did not get worse, but it also has not improved in the last three months.*

*Yes, this will be quite a marathon, and as any runner knows, training and discipline help determine the race. I say help, because we know that God's grace is sufficient to supply all we need. But we are told: "In the race, all the runners run, but only one gets the prize. Run in such a way as to get the prize" (1 Cor. 9:24).*

*So I solicit your earnest prayers in this, the longest and toughest leg of the race.*

*To God be the glory!*

*God Bless,*<br>*Alana*

As an ugly backdrop to these last few weeks, an old, buried, (but obviously not healed) wound had begun to throb. The relationship with my aunt from Florida had taken a turn for the worse. Ordinarily, a blow-off email would barely warrant mention, but with all we were going through, I was deeply hurt by the introduction of new strife. I was not ready to include that in an email (or talk about it to friends), so I masked it as the stress of the holidays.

With my mom having been gone for so long, I needed my aunts for maternal support. I hoped with the five of them, we would receive some emotional support. But time and again, I was disappointed. These new events collided with the memories of my mother's story, and I had to put a hold on finishing my memoir.

### *January 24, 2011: Starting Leg Rehab*

*One thing I am being reminded of repeatedly in this process is that God listens! He continues to hear your prayers for our son and for our family. We keep referring to*

Malcolm as the runner, and us as coaches, but most days, it feels like we run beside him, and you can see from my last update that I/we have been growing weary.

One of our fondest memories of running the Houston Half Marathon was of the crowds of people shouting our names, and encouraging us to keep going. None of them knew us personally, but they got up early in the morning, grabbed pom-poms, and read our names from our runner's bibs! The more tired a runner looks, the more strangers yell his name. Similarly, these past couple of weeks, we have received more encouragement, cheers, kind words, and company. The holidays are stressful enough as it is, but adding the hospital and the recent extended family turmoil, I was running on empty! Thank you!

I wanted to attach a picture, but Malcolm would kill me, so please allow me to just describe him. In a matter of a couple of weeks, his hair has grown back, complete with eyebrows, mustache and beard (he's always been proud of his chin patch). He has always had thick, black eyebrows against his medium cocoa skin, so their absence was very obvious, but so is their return. His thin frame is even thinner than at the start, but he is getting his color back (at one point, he looked a washed-out gray).

The hairs on his head are very fine, and remind me of a six-month old baby's hair, although Malcolm said it's already falling out again, from his chemo a week ago. Speaking of chemo, he just finished a week on a new medicine. It made him pretty sick, and his counts are still down. He'll have the next couple of weeks off, from a chemo standpoint, while he focuses on his physical therapy.

He's always been the kind of kid (now a man) who dismisses everything you say, but then when you're not looking, will do what you "encouraged" or insisted that he do. As a parent/coach it is frustrating, but it is his way of maintaining control (with or without cancer—remember high school?) So now, he has been rehabbing his leg his own way, and he's able to walk around with a limp. He can walk the entire house without crutches! He has a daily rehab schedule at MD Anderson, and he is now set up to get taxi rides. This helps him maintain his own control, and eases some of the burden of transporting him around! Such an answered prayer! Of course, we'll still go with him to doctor's visits, and chemo treatments.

So as we run this race with him, we have to remember: "Let us run with perseverance the race marked out for us, fixing our eyes on Jesus, the pioneer and perfecter of faith" (Heb. 12:1).

To God be the glory!

*God Bless,*
*Alana*

### February 9, 2011: Chemo Round Four

*Okay, here we go! It's chemo week, Round Four. The doctors started Malcolm on a new medicine after his surgery, because once they took the tumor out of his knee, they could be a bit smarter about his treatment. The results of that tumor analysis showed that it was seventy percent dead, which meant the other chemo drugs were okay, but that he needed something different, so that's where we are. This one makes the schedule a little easier, but it seems harder on his body. Before, he was only getting the chemo drug for a day, then other meds to help flush it out, followed by another drug for a day (about two weeks after the first). Now, he gets the chemo drug for an entire week! He will likely need a transfusion next week, as his platelets were low after the last round.*

*So aside from being sick for a week, Malcolm is actually making excellent progress on his physical therapy—his way! I was overjoyed when he walked up to the front door last week (on snow/ice day), as the boys were preparing to head to San Antonio with their mom to visit their sick grandfather. He apologized for being so distant and not returning my phone calls. I was getting really emotional about that distance, because our new-found understanding is still very fragile.*

*I can't begin to imagine what Malcolm is going through emotionally, and since he won't tell me, I guess I won't! I do know that he is trying to become a man, but as a mom I can't help worrying about him isolating himself. I pray against the spirit of depression, as he deals with the loss of his health at such a young age. I also pray that he turns away from the choices and habits he refuses to put down that have already brought so much turmoil to our family, and his own life. I know...not in MY time...*

*In other Hill family news, Marcus is still working at Kroger, and saving up for his car! On the other hand, if he doesn't get those grades up, he won't be able to drive it! Mason has made the transition into middle school (and has even gone to a couple of dances), and Matthew is preparing for his eighth birthday! He has his last basketball game this weekend, and he seems to have turned a corner with using the court as his emotional outlet for all of this. His mood swings have been even wilder than normal (and you know that's already wild). But when asked if he wanted to talk to me (or anyone for that matter), he responded, "Mommy, I'm a boy, and we don't like to talk about our feelings!" So from the baby, I know how to approach my oldest. Ain't life funny?*

*We have all been affected by Malcolm's battle with cancer, and display it in different ways. The biggest lesson we are getting from God now is this: "Above all else, love each other deeply, because love covers over a multitude of sins!" (1 Pet. 4:8).*

*He keeps teaching, and with faith, we keep learning! To God be the glory!*

*God Bless,*<br>*Alana*

# Chapter 8

## In the Crockpot

***February 23, 2011: CT scan shows a longer race***

I just can't get over God's lesson planning! All my teacher friends know, we wish we could tailor a lesson in such perfect timing as He does. By that, I'm referring to the sermon Pastor West preached this past Sunday (with Malcolm present, and eagerly listening). He referred to Matthew 14:22-33, when the disciples were in the boat, and Peter walked on water. Remember that story? Well, there were two important points to get from that: one, that *sometimes we get a storm BECAUSE we're obedient (Jesus **told** the disciples to go in the boat ahead of him); and two, that delay is not denial—Jesus came to the disciples in the **fourth** watch of the night.*

So why am I preaching in an email? Because today Malcolm went to MD Anderson for a CT scan, chest x-ray, and blood-work, all of which confirmed that there is still much left in this race. Our faith was tested with more facts. We spent the weekend celebrating life (Matt's eighth birthday), and listening to Mal (and us all) talk about what he is going to do this summer, when this is all over. We were even overjoyed that Matthew, while loving basketball, had asked to have a football party (complete with a game in the back yard). It's a shame that I was too busy entertaining to get pictures of Malcolm playing standing quarterback, complete with moves out of the pocket. Without saying a word to the kids at the party (all of whom know of his illness), he testified to the healing that is taking place in his body, and by being present for his little brother's birthday, he displayed the healing in his heart.

Today we were all reminded that God is in control, and often He heals (or "comes to us") in the early dawn, after we have waited for Him all night! Not shouting yet? Peter walked on water for a moment (was full of confidence), but then he got scared and took his eyes off Jesus ("saw the wind"), and when he did, he sank! That, friends, describes the emotions we have felt on this journey. When we are looking Jesus square in the eyes, we can see *this cancer going away, being defeated. But when we see the scans and the test results (and sometimes even talk to people), we take our eyes off of Him, and we get scared. Our spirits sink like Peter in the water, and we're left screaming for someone, anyone, to pull us back into the boat! Well, I'm glad you're in the boat with us, because you, too, will see the power of God when this storm is over!*

*The new storm shaking our boat is this: the tumors have not shrunk. The doctors plan to continue chemo for four to six more months, and THEN they plan to follow with a study chemo drug for six months after that, and THEN they will schedule lung surgery. So that's at least another year of chemo, as long as his kidneys can handle it. Boo! But it will be undeniable that it was the hand of God at work in HIS time. Yay!*

*To God be the glory for the shout in my spirit right now! Thanks for praying and reading!*

*God Bless,*
*Alana*

## February 23, 2011: CT scan shows a longer race, Part Two

*I don't usually do this, but this requires a part two, and the Holy Spirit won't let me keep it to myself. Really, it's not me!*

*Microwaves, ovens, and Crock-pots: a good cook*

knows which to use, and when, and so does God! He knows when to put blessings in the microwave, when to put them in the oven, and when to let them simmer in a Crock-pot. And the Bible is full of situations for each:

The three Hebrew boys who were rescued from the fiery furnace—microwave.

Hannah, who waited to conceive her son Samuel—oven.

Then there was Job and his long-suffering—in the Crock-pot.

Some of my favorite dishes are cooked in the Crock-pot, and we wait all day while the smell of the perfectly mixed and measured ingredients fills the house...oh!

As we deal with the fact that we're looking at another year (at least) before this Goliath goes down, I can't help but reflect on the other times God has had me wait. Each time was never to hurt me, but to make me stronger, to let my spirit "simmer" in His presence. I waited for God to heal me from the death of my mother. I waited for God to give me a family. I waited for God to give me a baby (yes, that order is correct). I waited for God to give me a business. And each time, the smell of that blessing brewing was almost as good as that first bite! Each of those was preparation to help me minister to my son (and myself) in this hour of waiting.

Two scriptures we're holding onto: "But they that wait upon the LORD shall renew their strength, they shall mount up with wings as eagles, they shall run and not be weary, *they shall walk and not faint" (Isa. 40:31); and "Many are the plans of man, but it is the purpose of the LORD that will stand" (Prov. 19:20-21).*

*Thank you LORD, for Your Word and Your perfect Will!*

*God Bless,*

*Alana*

# Chapter 9

## Lord, Help Us All

**March 23, 2011: Happy Birthday Mal!**

I kept talking myself out of sending the angry updates that have been floating in my head these past few weeks. So allow me to summarize what has caused me so many sleepless nights (and delayed me sending an update). Just after preaching my first sermon to our youth about the microwave, oven and Crock-pot (inspired by my last update), the boy (as I call him when I'm angry), was so busy running the streets with his buddies that he didn't come home.

Now before you tell me, "he's a teenager," or "he's a young adult," allow me to remind you of the legal bills, sleepless nights, jail visits, sadness, and depression we all felt when he was on the streets before. And let me also be clear that he doesn't just hang out—he smokes (not Marlboros), and disrespects, and disregards his mother, brothers, and us! It is increasingly disheartening to minister to youth at my church, when my own won't straighten up. I get that kids will make mistakes, and my lovelies in ministry aren't angels! There is also the obvious issue of fighting to save your life from cancer, all the while killing yourself with poor choices...oh, the irony!

We battled feelings of anger, resentment, disappointment, and frustration. The parable of the Prodigal Son prepared us for what to do as parents when he returned, and we did just that—we rejoiced to the highest! We asked very few questions, and while he smelled like a pig, we embraced him with open arms. What that story didn't prepare us for, was the poop-head leaving again. In the story, the son returns, repents of his ways, and the family celebrates—end of story.

Well, we found out there was no true repentance, only a hiding of ways. We were brokenhearted—again! So this now has become less about forgiving the lost son, and more about forgiving time and again, and we know that's a LOT harder!

It's already hard to take your hands off your kids when

*they grow up, but we spend years preparing for that, and trust me, we had done just that. But how do you do that, when he is also battling a life-threatening illness? I shared that his last doctor's appointment didn't show much progress, and that we would be fighting this a lot longer. What I didn't share is that the doctor's "survival-rate talk" has drastically increased again. We face the reality of losing our son each and every day. He is trying to cope with this reality in his own way, but knowing that fact doesn't make it any easier to watch.*

*Well, today is his birthday, and I can't think of a better reason to put all the stuff I just mentioned above into the closet. To celebrate, we dragged him over here, gave him a cupcake cake with a smiley face on it, and grilled burgers. If it weren't for the chemo bag he was carrying, you'd think it was just another birthday. Don't take my word for it. Look at the attached pictures! I love that God loves us enough to keep shining His light, even in the darkest of situations.*

*Happy nineteenth birthday, Malcolm! We pray for many more. We love you! Sucks to be on chemo on your birthday, but we are so thankful to God that you are celebrating another birthday!*

*On another, equally sad, note, I returned from a youth retreat this past weekend to find that my beloved pet bird Buster had died. I got him fifteen years ago when he was just a baby. He was the child I brought into the marriage. I showed the kids the pictures I had taken over the years of Buster perching on their heads, and that brought levity to the situation, but he will be missed around here! We had a funeral for him in the backyard, and as sad as that was, we were so grateful to be burying our bird, and not our child.*

*Thanks again for being part of our family journey.*

*God Bless,*

*Alana*

This birthday was also important for us because Malcolm chose to celebrate his last two birthdays alone. And while we stop giving the boys parties at ten (usually going out to dinner or something instead), it was nice to make a big fuss, given that a birthday for a cancer patient is a victory in and of itself. The doctor had begun saying his cancer wasn't responding to the chemo, so those visits were getting scarier.

During his divorce, Rodney had insisted on the most liberal visitation he could get, so we had the boys about half the time. But at seventeen years old, Malcolm's rebellion intensified, and we resolved for the time being to keep him away from his siblings. Besides, he kept running away, and he was stressing out our entire family.

We were angry and disappointed, but his behavior was really taking a toll on his younger brothers. Marcus was trying to establish himself in high school, and was missing the closeness he had once shared with his big brother. Mason innocently looked up to his oldest brother, hanging onto every word he said. While it was sweet that he was so supportive, as parents we worried that he could too easily follow an example that he seemed to lovingly justify. And then there was Matthew, his baby brother (eleven years his junior). From the moment he was old enough to do so, Malcolm could always be found holding his youngest brother in his arms or lap. The two looked identical, despite having different mothers.

For months, all we could do was cry and pray, and encourage ourselves in the Word. Some of our friends couldn't understand the pain we were in, or why we were so angry. When one of us would get discouraged about his absence (or the latest court appearance), we would look at the other and say, "He'll be back…God will bring him back." That was a statement we had to repeat numerous times before we could believe it, but even just saying it turned our attention away from what he was currently doing, and onto what he would be doing. It reminded us that God speaks life into dead situations, and so should we. Some days were easier than others, and we spent more than our fair share of time venting and complaining about his radically defiant behavior. I tried unsuccessfully to detach myself, insisting that he was not "my child," but my heart would not let me. Reading an email from a friend one day, I received the Word from Ecclesiastes 7:13: "Consider what God has done: Who can straighten what he has made crooked?"

### March 29, 2011: Chemo Round Five, Part One

These email are getting harder and harder to write, not just because of the emotions of having a sick "child" (okay, he's nineteen), but because of the conflict we feel needing to love someone from afar, but caring enough to help him live. But like an athlete who has trained hard for an event, I know the Lord has been preparing us for this for years. And because of His overwhelming love for us, we will have all we need to get through this. "But my God shall supply all your needs according to his riches in glory by Christ Jesus" (Phil. 4:19).

We made a decision when we first got Malcolm's diagnosis that we would not operate in fear, but that we would stand strong on God's promise. But watching him go through this brings back painful memories for our family, specifically for my husband. The first few years of our marriage, we attended several funerals for family members; one was for a cousin my age. The most painful, however, was the loss of Rodney's dad in 2004.

### April 1, 2011: Chemo Round 5, Part two

I am actually writing part of this while sitting in the waiting room at MD Anderson. Malcolm almost missed his appointment for blood work yesterday , and he was making no effort to get here for his blood transfusion. But God *amazingly sent me another mom to talk to. Her son, Tre, is sixteen and also has osteosarcoma, and he was such a beacon of light, as he sat in his wheelchair without his left leg! As I talked to his mom, I suddenly felt normal for having moments of despair, followed by moments of complete hope, followed by moments of nothing. Just today alone, I have experienced about eight different emotions, ranging from enthusiasm to homicidal! I'm too young for the change of life, so I know that's not it. We can't change the storm, or decide when it will be over, so I'm just praying, and asking God to give me peace while it is here, and I'll throw in a hallelujah anyhow!*

*I've had people ask me if Malcolm has given up. On the contrary, he's just ready for it to be over, so he can get back to doing nothing. Not the answer I was hoping for when I asked him the question, but he is at least now being honest about his lack of ambition (instead of faking goals).*

*And as you can imagine, the treatment plan has changed again. He now has only one more round of chemo, followed by recovery. Then they will schedule his lung surgery for late June or early July. From there, they will see if the cancer cells are dead (scans still show nodes, but they could be dead nodes), and if so, he will be declared to be in remission. If not, they will continue with some alternative treatments. Either way, it will be a long and painful recovery from that surgery!*

*So for now, we are gearing up for our cruise this summer from New Orleans. That will be a time for us to get away from the drama surrounding Malcolm personally, and the uncertainty surrounding him medically. We're going on our cruise before his surgery, and Mason and Matthew are really looking forward to it. Marcus will be working, unfortunately, so won't be going with us.*

*As always, thanks for taking this journey with us, and thanks for your prayers. We could not have made it without the love of our Lord and Savior, and the support of our friends and family.*

*God Bless,*
*Alana*

And there we were, trying to focus on moving forward, and yet Malcolm's past behaviors were resurfacing, entering the present, and forcing us to practice mercy…again. Finding myself wondering, "When will he ever learn?" I felt myself grow frustrated and distant again.

Rodney and I were barely speaking to Malcolm, making our assigned trips to the hospital with him in silence. On this last visit with me, he wanted to continue to debate the harmlessness his actions, and I refused to have that conversation with him. After he told me again how it doesn't hurt anybody, I became suddenly furious. I yelled, and reminded him of the legal fees, time away from work, and overall stress that it has put on our family for years. I instantly regretted my angry response, and use of expletives, so I continued the trip in silence. I felt my heart hardening, and I was frustrated with myself. We were not just fighting his cancer, we were battling the strongholds that kept our son from being all that God has called him to be and it hurt.

And despite many cries to our pastor to get spiritual and emotional support for Malcolm and for us, our church was too busy. We didn't receive visits, or calls in the hospital when Malcolm had his leg surgery, and for the sake of ministry, I had to let it go. But as the diagnosis seemed to worsen, and we found ourselves in need, we were disheartened that our church wasn't there. Being a caregiver for someone with cancer, especially someone who is acting out, is an emotionally exhausting experience, and we would have welcomed the support of ministry.

There were days of complete hopelessness where I cried until my back hurt, and my eyes swelled shut. This is what depression feels like, and it hurt all over (just like the commercial says). Once, I couldn't get through lunch with a friend, because I began sobbing uncontrollably, at this point totally distraught over the absence of my aunts, whom I needed desperately.

Finally, overwhelmed by Malcolm's illness and defiance, and physically and emotionally exhausted from trying to keep it all together, I arranged to speak to a minister at church. After just five minutes in her office, the floodgates opened, and my cries could be heard across the building. If I shed one more tear, I was going to demand a prescription of some sort. But I didn't even have time to see a therapist to get one!

I spent the next day venting, crying, praying, and praising (in that order), until God restored my spirit, and helped me start to move on. I was clearly battling the spirit of depression, and up until that day, it was winning. His word began to flow from my heart, reminding me that HE is all I need. *"Find rest, O my soul, in God alone; my hope comes from him" (Pss. 62:5).*

I was still deeply wounded inside by the absence of family, but I decided to deal with that later. My nervous breakdown was going to have to wait! From the moment we got Malcolm's diagnosis, I began to ask people to pray for us. I needed strength, and while intercessory prayer is important, I knew that I was going to have to pray for myself, too. I had to manage my expectations, and not fall apart when I was disappointed. Feeling alone and "forsaken," I threw myself at the Master's feet, where I should have been all along! *"Let us then approach the throne of grace with confidence, so that we may receive mercy and find grace to help us in our time of need" (Heb. 4:16).*

### *April 21, 2011: Lung Surgery Scheduled*

*Well, we started the 2010-2011 school year with the news that Malcolm had cancer. I guess it is fitting to end it with his final surgery (and hopefully the words that he is cancer-free). Lung surgery has now been scheduled for Wednesday May 25, at MD Anderson. Between now and then, Malcolm has been instructed to eat well, continue his physical therapy, and refrain from anything that might keep him from bringing his platelet count up. To put it in perspective, his count is only thirty-seven thousand, and it should be between eighty and a hundred thousand, so for that reason they have stopped his chemo treatments, just one short of the planned end, but he was excited to get that news last week! So we get to enjoy Easter and the next few weeks, to help wind down the school year (and get some work done).*

*We met with his oncologist and surgeon on Wednesday to get all the details about the surgery, including which lung (the right) they will be operating on. I'll spare you all the gory details, but just know it's going to hurt—a lot— because they actually take out his lung! Once they remove the twelve or so nodes they found on the scans, they will send the nodes to pathology to determine if they still contain cancer cells. If they are clear, then he is in remission, and the celebrations begin! But if cancer is found, they will put Malcolm on an experimental treatment for nine months.*

*In the words of the great musician, Lisa Lisa, I'm all cried out, and I need this to be over!"*

*The words, "This too shall pass," have brought us very little comfort, but knowing that while we are yet in the storm, God loves us and is in the storm with us—now that's comfort!*

*Happy Easter! He is RISEN!*

*God Bless,*

*Alana*

Easter is supposed to be a time of celebration for our risen Savior. It is THE most important and cherished day on a Christian's calendar. I was in youth ministry leadership, and chose to remain active even after the diagnosis, so this was an especially busy time.

Serving God by serving His people helped lift the dark clouds. The darkness made way for light, and I was beginning to feel like myself again. I began to look ahead to the victory, instead of gazing behind at the battle. To encourage us on the remaining leg of the race, I booked us on a cruise for next year, on a grand new ship, and invited our friends and family to join us.

## Chapter 10

## Are We There Yet?

***May 9, 2011: Happy Mother's Day***

Despite the beautiful spring weather, these past couple of months have been the most emotional on our journey thus far. Friendly calls have lessened, and feelings of sadness, isolation, and exhaustion prevailed. But God! There is nothing like basking in the glory of our Father in Heaven to give us our strength and perspective back.

Like Job, who endured great loss, our family

*(individually and collectively) has continued to honor and praise God in our trial. But as we did, the enemy's attacks got stronger and more hurtful. He began with an attack on my child's body, taking his health from him, but then he continued with an attack on his mind (encouraging him to return to past destructive behaviors). But the enemy wasn't satisfied! He continued by attacking relationships, and more dangerously, the cunning serpent began raising doubts and stirring confusion at church!*

*And when the enemy could not get us with destruction, he tried to get us with distraction! But this past weekend, we got to see an encore performance from God as he brought ALL my boys together to celebrate Mother's Day with me (on Saturday evening—that's Stepmother's Day). The highlight was Marcus telling a joke, and Matthew being giddy all through dinner because he got to sit by his big brother!*

*As a mom, I have learned that we can sometimes learn the best lessons (and get the funniest stories) from watching our kids, especially when they're small. Matthew (or "Lil Man" as we call him), decided when he learned to walk, that he was going to be a basketball player. He works tirelessly at his craft, and has excelled to the point where he can hit an NCAA three-pointer with little effort! But that's not the funny story. Once, at school, a little boy was taunting him, telling him how badly he was going to beat him in basketball. Without hesitation, Matthew got the ball from the bully, and began dribbling around him. He then took two no-look jump shots over the boy (much like he did against a high-schooler at a recent church function).*

*But the best part of the story was hearing him tell me that he has such an unshakeable confidence in the gift that God has given him, that even his "enemies" could not shake him! And Matthew knows first-hand that he needs his haters; they are the best opponents, and make you bring your A-game! But he also knows that he doesn't have to agree with what they say about him, and he knows that when God is for you, no one can be against you!*

*Watching my children flourish in this situation has brought me the greatest joy. Through this trial, God is building empathy in my children for others who have sickness in their families. He is teaching them how to pray for others, and just as importantly, how to pray for themselves. As this goes on, the Words in the Bible come off the page, and become real to them (and me), and they can say they learned to pray and praise, just like David did!*

*So as we try to preserve our emotional and physical energy for the hill we must climb next, we are forever grateful for the prayers, thoughts, cheers, emails, texts, and Facebook posts that have helped encourage us. But mostly, we are thankful to God our Father for sustaining us with His loving grace—because His grace is sufficient!*

*Malcolm's lung surgery is still scheduled for Wednesday, May 25, and today he has his final appointment* with the surgeon who operated on his leg. And like Jason Terry (of the Dallas Mavericks) said, when asked how they swept the Lakers, "TO GOD BE THE GLORY!"

God Bless,<br>Alana

### May 24, 2011: Surgery Tomorrow!

Well, here we go! This is the day we've been waiting for with much anticipation, the day of Malcolm's lung surgery. They told us in the beginning that this would need to happen, but they weren't sure when. We do know this marks an important milestone in our journey. We sat and waited, while he went in for surgery to remove the tumor in his leg in December, praying and hoping that the doctors would not have to amputate. God did it! Not only was his leg spared, but Malcolm now walks without a hint of a limp! He even joined in the family basketball tournament we had this past Saturday in celebration of Rodney's and Marcus's birthdays.

As he gave me a sweaty good-bye hug, I couldn't help but pause, and thank God not just for him being at the birthday party (because that was a move of God itself), but for him to be able to participate in such an active event. Well, we know He is an encore God, so we are looking for Him to do it again!

We have so many examples of His favor, because as I

type this, a contractor is surveying our home to repair the water damage we got on Saturday morning, when a pipe in our kitchen burst! Yes, that enemy is crafty, but he can't keep us down! Our walls and baseboards in the kitchen, living room, and part of the hall will need to be repaired and painted, but thank God for insurance. Not something we wanted to deal with the week of surgery, but it could have been worse. I just wish I had time to pick out the new paint!

So, surgery is tomorrow morning. Malcolm has to be at MD Anderson at six-thirty in the morning, but we're not sure when they'll call him for surgery. As a matter of fact, he's heading there now to get another scan, because the doctors just realized he needed one. Uh, really? His platelets are up, and his body is ready for surgery. He has admitted that he's nervous, and I can only imagine, because I know we are too, and it's not our body! Plus, there is the waiting to hear what the pathology says: all clear? Or more chemo? I'll do my best to send an update when we get one at the hospital. We are praying not just for healing, but for WHOLENESS! To God be the glory!

Thanks for your prayers, and your cheers. GO TEAM MALCOLM!

*God Bless,*
*Alana*

### *May 31, 2011: Surgery went well, thanks!*

When you walk through something as uncertain as lung surgery, it's easier to not walk alone. On behalf of my entire family, I want to extend a warm thank you for walking alongside us. Our faith in God lets us know that we are never alone, and that He will never leave us nor forsake us, but there is something heartwarming in having friends and family (and sometimes near strangers) praying with you, and encouraging you along the way!

We arrived at the hospital early Wednesday morning for Malcolm's surgery. I actually joined a friend's work carpool so I could get Matt off to school first, while Coach Dad headed in earlier to be there by six-thirty. When I got to the hospital about an hour later, Mal was still in the waiting area, so I had a chance to see him quickly. He was called back shortly after that, and I set up camp in the waiting room for the long day ahead. He was eager when I went back to see him, and ready to get the whole thing over with, laughing and pointing at the magic marker on his right lung that read "YES." Surgery began at about nine-thirty.

Heaven was bombarded with his name, as prayer warriors arrived at the hospital praying, and I received texts, some simply saying "Praying now." We knew God was scrubbing up for surgery! In what seemed like no time, we were being called back for an update. Time seemed to fly *this time, partly because we could watch comedy shows on Coach Dad's new iPad, and partly because it really was a quick surgery. At twelve-thirty, we talked to the surgeon, and she told us she was done, and that surgery went well. She noted that Malcolm "looked good," and that she had cancelled his ICU bed—all great news! She did point out that he had some air bubbles and black spots on his lungs, in addition to the fourteen nodules she had carefully removed.*

*With this wonderful news, we happily high-fived everyone we could find, and we waited to be able to see Malcolm in recovery. That wait took the longest, and once we did get to see him, it was almost like seeing a baby in the NICU. With his new baby-fine hair, Malcolm really looked the part. While he slept peacefully, I rubbed his head, kissed him, and reminded him that he's my favorite (especially when he's under anesthesia!)*

*So we waited the rest of the day. We finally left the hospital about seven in the evening, and Malcolm still hadn't been moved to his room. He got moved a little later, and we spent the next couple of days visiting, and checking on his progress. Surprisingly, Thursday's visit found him sitting in the chair, being witty—a nice by-product of an epidural. The next day was more of the same. Saturday, they removed the epidural, and told him he might go home on Monday, but when we visited him Sunday, the pain in his body, and the disappointment of not going home as soon as he thought he might, made him a very unpleasant patient. He dug his heels in, and refused the nurse's orders, barking at her, and insisting that we not ask either. He did, however, draw with Matthew. Matthew will carry that Captain America picture around with him for years to come! Sunday's visit was about the same, and I just kept my head down, and prayed that Malcolm would find peace.*

*So now it looks like he might come home Wednesday, but that depends on how cooperative he is! We should find out by the end of the week whether or not the nodules they removed are still cancerous, or dead cancer cells killed by the chemo! Right now we are also focused on getting everyone through the remainder of the school year, and finishing on a high note! All the boys had improved their grades, even in the midst of the storm! To God be the glory!*

*God Bless,*

*Alana*

## Chapter 11

## Staying for the Encore

***June 3, 2011: Malcolm coming home from the hospital***

*It has been such a roller-coaster week around here. First, the doctors told Malcolm he might go home Monday. Then they took some more chest x-rays, and found an air pocket near his chest tube. The doctor explained that this would heal on its own, and that Malcolm needed to walk, and give it a couple of days. Malcolm was so disappointed* at not going home, that he refused to walk, or do anything else the doctor advised.

By Wednesday, the doctors had taken more x-rays (this was a morning routine), and they found several air pockets, and commented that his lungs were not reconnecting to his chest walls. This was potentially dangerous, a condition that could lead to a collapsed lung, so they ordered him to remain for another five days. Coach Dad was with him (and relayed this news to me,) but noted that Malcolm was taking it in stride. I guess he had done enough pouting on Tuesday. I can relate! You give yourself a pouting-budget, and just don't go over it.

So, Friday morning came, Malcolm called and said, "Guess what? I'm coming home today!" So as I write this, the doctors have removed the tube from his chest, and he has packed his things. I decided to wait until he was walking to the car to hit send...so here I go! The doctors told us to check back Monday on the pathology results to see if the cancer is gone, and we believe it, in Jesus' name! I'll send confirmation as soon as we get it!

*God Bless,*
*Alana*

### *June 7, 2011: PRAISE REPORT!*

*We just got the news from the doctor's office. GOD DID IT AGAIN! Malcolm is CANCER FREE! I can barely sit still to type this. My soul is sooo happy!*

*Nine months ago when we first started this journey, we began to pray and ask you to join us in praying. Today, our prayers have been answered! We go to MD Anderson one last time tomorrow morning, for his blood-work, and to ring the cancer-survivor bell! We praise God, from whom all blessings flow!!*

*Malcolm came home from the hospital Friday evening with a renewed sense of gratitude, having had to stay in a few extra days. We went to see* X-Men *early Saturday morning, followed by burgers for lunch, a Hill family fave! On the drive back home, Malcolm told us how he met a seventeen-year-old boy who was down the hall from him. He was recently diagnosed with osteosarcoma in his right leg (same as Malcolm), and he was starting his first round of chemo. Malcolm talked to him about what to expect, and they exchanged numbers so they could stay in touch.*

*Please remember, Malcolm had been refusing to walk, or follow doctor's orders. When the nurses told him about the boy, he walked straight out of his room, and down the hall. He even walked his mom to her car! I was so proud to hear him talking about the opportunity to be there for someone, and I praised God for moving in his heart and* revealing His purpose. We know Malcolm still has areas to grow in, and some things he needs to put down, but for right now, we are going to shout, and praise the growth that we have seen these past few months.

We serve a MIGHTY GOD who is bigger than any cancer, or bad attitude! Thanking Him for HEALING. Believing Him for WHOLENESS! Amen!

To God be the Glory!

God Bless,
Alana

### July 7, 2011: Looking Ahead

It's hard to believe it's been a month since my last email telling you that Malcolm was cancer-free, and so much has happened since then! We rang the bell at MD Anderson celebrating the end of his treatments, although we still had an appointment with his oncologist. His doctor was excited about his progress, but also had to give him the sobering report that his years of smoking had done major damage to his lungs. Malcolm bucked and mouthed off, and I dropped my head and gave him and his attitude to God. (Yes, we have all grown in this process!) He will need to have scans every three months for the first couple of years, then with less frequency.

While still basking in the "after-cancer" glow,

*Matthew, Mason, Dad, and I boarded the Carnival Conquest for our last cruise on that vessel. (She's moving to a different port after this summer.) I was able to again visit the land of my mother's birth (Jamaica), and I spent my birthday on a horse in the Cayman Islands (the land of my grandmother's birth). Both these visits helped ease the sting of reaching the age my mom had been when she died—thirty-nine. The kids had a great time, and their present to me was no bickering in the cabin, which they maintained for seven whole days! See, there IS a God!*

*Meanwhile, back home, Marcus had saved up his money, and bought himself a car. We returned to Houston on Father's Day, met my Dad for brunch in town, and then came home. Malcolm decided he wanted to walk over, obviously thankful for the activity of his limbs because it was a mile and a half, and a hundred degrees! He arrived wearing a wide-brimmed hat, and carrying a water bottle. His newly grown hair was curled from the sweat, looking like a baby's after a bath. What a sight! Then a little later, Marcus drove over in his car, and he proudly showed off the car's big trunk! The best part was watching my husband visit with ALL his boys on Father's Day—to God be the Glory!*

*But wait, I'm not done! Last week, Malcolm came over to fill out college financial aid forms! He wants to learn a trade, and get a stable job, words that are like music to our ears. Oh, and there's more. Just the other night, we all had dinner together (always a big deal when your kids get older, especially in a blended family), and then, in the parking lot, Malcolm demonstrated his new ability to jog. Just last week, he had his chest port removed. His hair, mustache and beard are all back, so we all cheered him on, and thanked God for restoration! Malcolm plans to enter college in the fall, and we could not be more proud of his new attitude. "And we know that in all things God works for the good of those who love him, who have been called according to his purpose" (Rom. 8:28).*

*And finally, we have officially begun to train for the Houston Half Marathon on January 15, 2012 as we RUN FOR A REASON. We are more than conquerors through Christ Jesus, and we pray that you'll partner with us by donating to our fundraising campaign. Malcolm will be cheering us on from the sidelines, as he is now fully aware of the grace God has given him! I pray that you will be able to join him.*

*"I do not consider myself yet to have taken hold of it. But one thing I do: Forgetting what is behind and straining toward what is ahead, I press on toward the goal to win the prize for which God has called me heavenward in Christ Jesus" (Phil. 3:13-14).*

*Thanks again for all the support and prayers.*

*God Bless,*

*Alana*

Ringing the cancer-free bell at the hospital was a day we had anticipated for months. Since I was registered (and had paid for) a professional conference, I had to leave right after the appointment. I arrived at the conference with a button about Cancer Survivor Day and a huge smile on my face. I spent more time testifying to colleagues about the goodness of God in healing my son than on project management. I even met a woman who recently wrote a book about her child having cancer and we shared our stories. There I had been planning a book on my journey to adulthood, when I realized I had a more important story to tell first.

# Chapter 12

## Analyzing the Results

**July 29, 2011: Joy and Pain**

"Joy and pain, it's like sunshine and rain..." Maze put it best, and we quote it often. These past couple of weeks have been filled with that mix of emotion. We are celebrating, and so proud of Malcolm's attitude and progress. He has enrolled in college (he'll be attending community college starting next month), and he is about to get his driver's license. Yes, he is becoming a man! That is the JOY. The pain, however, is that on Monday, his friend and mentor in bone cancer, Brent Weaver, passed away. We were deeply saddened by the news.

If you recall, we participated in a charity walk for him, and Brent was very supportive of Malcolm during his treatments and surgery, letting him know what to expect, and encouraging him to stay the course. My immediate concern upon hearing the news was first for his sweet wife, but secondly, I hoped this doesn't discourage Malcolm from living, and moving forward with his life. The ugly truth about cancer is that it has a tendency to come back, and in Brent's case, the recurrence was just as severe as the initial case that had cost him his leg.

Malcolm has his first post-treatment scan in a couple of weeks (August 8), and while we want him to be diligent about his care, we don't want him looking over his shoulder for the rest of his life. Thankfully God continues to send him (and us) long-time survivors to inspire and encourage him. So instead of freaking out and harping on fear, we all see this as another reason to be thankful for God's grace in Malcolm's life! And thankfully, he shares that sentiment. We have watched the enemy set a trap for our son, but we are so thankful that the enemy's weapon can become God's tool for our good, and His glory!!

As Job said to the LORD after questioning Him, and hearing His response: "I know you can do all things, no *plan of yours can be thwarted" (Job 42:2). To God be the glory!*

*God Bless,*

*Alana*

### August 11, 2011: First Post-Treatment Scans

Wow, it was almost a year ago today that we got the devastating news of Malcolm's illness, but since then God has restored him and our family to better than we were before. Malcolm has the most beautiful head of curly brown hair, and we have not had this much harmony in our blended family since...ever!

Malcolm just had his first series of post-treatment scans, which consist of being x-rayed and prodded for a full day at MD Anderson. He and Coach Dad passed the time by watching movies, talking, and laughing; an update that was music to my ears, since on the last few trips, we had been just angry taxi drivers. As usual though, our celebrations were interrupted by his addiction. I am not going to call it a habit or activity, because that belittles its severity (although we say that at home, to keep from saying the a-word). This recent scan shows "something new" on his right lung. The left is still clear, and that is the side they operated on.

His medical team reminded him that he is causing major damage to his lungs by smoking, and that if they see more "something new" on his scans, they will have to do surgery on the right side. Since the pain and discomfort of *that procedure are still fresh in his mind, Malcolm actually agreed for the first time to quit. Now we're back to celebrating, because he has NEVER spoken these words...shouting yet! He doesn't realize it, but he's going to need help doing this, so I welcome any referrals or suggestions.*

*But this is the same kid that doctors said would never run again, and he decided to prove them wrong by sprinting down the street last week. Sure, he fell and scraped his hands, but he was so proud that he ran at all, he couldn't wait to rub it in the doctor's face! (Of course, the doctors reminded him of the danger of breaking that leg.) So I know once he puts his mind to breaking the strongholds in his life, he will emerge victorious again! The garage where he hung out is now spotless, and stores his mom's new car. He is going to use her old minivan to get himself to school, once it starts in a couple of weeks. Praising God for progress, but still praying for deliverance!*

*Speaking of running (and progress), we are really gearing up for our race. We're almost done with INSANITY which we are using as our pre-season training, and boy, is it whipping us into shape! If you are able, please make a donation to Young Texans Against Cancer.*

*Oh, and the book is coming along very well. Thanks for the encouragement, and stay tuned!*

*God Bless,*
*Alana*

# Chapter 13

## A Watched Pot Never Boils

***October 27, 2011: Look Out on the Roads!***

Can you believe it? Now there are two Hill boys with driver's licenses, terrorizing the streets of Sugar Land! Yes, Malcolm is now a licensed driver! He has been applying for jobs, and has decided to start school in January. We really hope he means it. I guess time will tell.

He had his second set of post-treatment scans and workups on Monday, and everything looks good. I suspect *he's had a wait-and-see attitude towards his healing, and that may have held him back from moving forward with his life. I hope that is the case. God knows we'd love to discover some sort of reason for his "nothingness." Playing video games should be a hobby, not a full-time endeavor, but I digress. Maybe with some facts to back his faith, he can press on!*

*Perspective is a lesson hard to teach kids. They have to see it for themselves, and our three younger boys were truly thankful to be starting a school year without the situation we had last year. They have a new-found empathy for families dealing with illness. Now, Marcus, Mason, and Matthew are all in the full swing of school. Marcus started with a strong showing. Mason fizzed out after the first couple of weeks, and quit the football team (but we were thrilled to see him on the field). Matthew brought home another set of straight A's. We are proud of all our boys, and are eager to see what this school year will bring them academically, emotionally, and spiritually. Oh, speaking of emotions, Mason will be thirteen next week, the newest Hill teenager. God give us strength!*

*Thanks for keeping us in your prayers. We're very close to our fundraising goal for the Houston Half Marathon, and thanks to all who supported.*

*God Bless,*
*Alana*

### February 6, 2012: The End of the Story?

*The year has been so busy that I haven't had a chance to put events into words until now. Sorry, but this email will be a long one!*

*At one of Matthew's Upward basketball games (the first one in January), I shared the half-time devotional, summarizing our testimony, and how God had used cancer to bring our son back, and to teach us how to love and forgive. I shared, "And we know that in all things God works for the good of those who love him, who have been called according to his purpose" (Rom. 8:28). What I didn't realize when I prepared to speak, was that Malcolm would be at the game (he hadn't been to one before then), and I did not know how he would feel about my speaking publicly about his illness and recovery. I took the microphone nervously, hoping he wouldn't be uncomfortable, and I completed the six-minute talk without crying (that was hard). When I had finished, I walked over to my family, and Malcolm grabbed me, and hugged me harder than he had ever done, and he said "Thank you. That was great." I was speechless. Thank you, God! And to think that I had wrestled with God that morning about what I should talk about. To God be the Glory!*

*Malcolm is cancer-free, seven months and counting,*

and is now a college student! (His first day of class was Tuesday, January 17.) He has taken his first test, and is thoroughly enjoying himself. He is going regularly for his scans, and is continuing to get the all-clear from his doctors. He has spent more time with us these past few weeks than he has in a long time, and we all love that. He has cut off some old friends who brought him back into bad habits. It is nice to see him happy and socializing. He even joined us for a Super Bowl party yesterday with a friend whose husband is also a recent cancer survivor.

Another highlight of January was running in the Houston Half Marathon. The IT Band Syndrome I had been struggling with did not bother me at all, and I was able to run my fastest time ever: two hours and fourteen minutes! Rodney and I finished together. We felt so good after the race that we actually walked around Discovery Green for a while with my Dad and the boys who came down to cheer us on. Malcolm overslept, but apologized later that day...wow! And as if that wasn't enough, Rodney ran another half marathon two weeks later, and finished in one hour and fifty-five minutes, proving that he really holds back to run with me. Such a sweetheart!

Running that race together and raising money for cancer research and awareness the weekend after Malcolm started his college classes, made for a wonderful ending to this incredible story. Just like the stories in the Bible that we read to learn more about God's will and His ways, I pray *that this story might not just encourage its readers, but serve as another account of God's grace. The crucial lessons we learned along the way, were worth the battle. Lesson one was about love: I never knew how to love like this! Lesson two was about fortitude: we can't have the TESTIMONY without the TEST.*

*To everything there is a season, and as we enter this new season, we are thankful for the people whom God has placed in our lives. At the end of the year, we decided to move from the church where we have been for the past twelve years. Just as Abraham had to be obedient to God, and move to Canaan to receive his blessing, we too will be moving, likely to a church in our community, where we can continue what was started at the Church Without Walls. There, I rededicated my life to Christ. There, my husband and my youngest were baptized. There, our older boys grew into teens, and worshiped like men. For those reasons, it will always have a special place in our hearts.*

*So as we move forward, we will also be dedicating a host of time to Matthew's first love: basketball. He will have his first AAU Tournament this weekend, and we are all excited to sit as a family during his games, cheering him on to victory, just as we did with Malcolm in his battle against cancer. The Hill family has emerged stronger, and with a greater faith than we ever thought possible: "Because we know that the testing of your faith produces perseverance" (James 1:3).*

*Thanks again for walking this faith-walk with us. We have appreciated every note, email, Facebook post, call, or text during this journey. You are forever a part of this story*

*God Bless,*

*Alana*

# Chapter 14

## Conclusion

**May 21, 2012: Anniversary is approaching**

*I stopped sending these emails regularly, because I didn't want to annoy anyone, but joy is infectious, and I want to sneeze on you for a minute! My spirits are soaring so high today, because yesterday we celebrated Marcus's eighteenth birthday, a major milestone in the life of any child. And since his birthday comes just nine days before his high school graduation, it also marks his official walk out of adolescence, and into manhood.*

*He hasn't always made the highest grades, and because he didn't get in as much trouble as his brother, he didn't see the problem; yet to see him persevere as he nears this finish line gives Rodney and me both a sense of pride as parents. We ask your prayers now, as he begins to make adult decisions, the first of which for him is whether or not to enter the Marine Corps, a desire he strongly expressed to us at brunch yesterday.*

*While I wanted to make sure I gave Marcus first mention, it was the latest chest scans for Malcolm that brought me to my computer. I held my breath a little this morning, praying that he would be able to celebrate his first year of being cancer-free. The doctors confirmed it, noting no changes in his lungs! Malcolm's recovery has been amazing, and he even plays basketball and paintball. He even bought himself a new paintball gun, which he shows off proudly. I am also happy to report that he just finished his first semester in college—and with flying colors! He has decided to be (and is applying himself towards becoming) an art teacher! Oh, how he will bless the lives of some youngsters in the near future! God is so amazing!*

*These two give Mason (now thirteen) and Matthew (now nine) some amazing examples and that is all you can ever ask for: examples of big hearts, and small mistakes; of giving up, and pushing through. In three weeks, we board a ship for our first-ever cruise as a complete family. (When we went two years ago, Malcolm chose not to join us.) I just might shout myself off the balcony!*

## Conclusion

*So if you thought miracles only happened in the Bible, I encourage you to look around. God is still in the miracle business! And not because we are so good and so faithful, but because HE is!*

*To God be the glory!!*

*God Bless,*

*Alana*

Just when we thought things couldn't get any better, we had a big backyard bash to celebrate our three major milestones: my fortieth birthday; Marcus' high school graduation; and Malcolm being one year cancer-free. The fourth, unspoken, milestone we celebrated that day was the reconciliation of our family. Friends and family joined us as we transformed our yard into a Jamaican paradise, complete with a sunset view! I honored my aunts with roses, thanking them for being there. My aunt from Florida had moved back to Houston, and was feeling like her old self again. When I prayed for God to heal my family, I was usually asking about my immediate family (too afraid to ask for too much), but He knew what I really needed.

Once a year, for the past four years, Rodney, Matthew and I would go on a cruise. We simply couldn't afford to go with all six of us, and as a result of being blended, we had to accept that sometimes we were three, and sometimes we were six. We did, however, always insist on having a family vacation with all of us, but it was usually a trip involving less expense.

For our tenth anniversary, just before learning of Malcolm's illness, we had saved, planning on a cruise for all of us—or rather, as it turned out, almost all of us. Malcolm did not consider himself part of our family at that time, so we were only five on that cruise. That was very disappointing, because we had worked hard (and prayed even harder) to bring our family of six back together, and to put the past behind us, but it wasn't the time yet

So with great excitement and some angst, we boarded the ship for seven days of fun and togetherness. We nervously invited Malcolm on the trip, fearing his rejection, and/or potentially poor behavior on board, as either one would be a setback. But to our pleasant surprise, he graciously accepted, even thanked us several times. Then on board the ship, he was a perfect gentleman, and other than a little argument over dress socks with Marcus, the trip was without incident.

It was no surprise that the ship was brand new, and that its name was *Carnival Magic*. We stopped at every photo station we could (and they have lots on board the Fun Ships), all in an attempt to capture that moment in time. Malcolm and Marcus are now adults, and we don't expect to see them daily. The time has come for them to leave the nest, and it was always our hope as parental eagles, that they would fly away, and not fall to the ground and be swooped upon by vultures. From the time our children were able, my husband and I have been giving them flying lessons in the hopes that they would soar!

## Conclusion

Family and relationships are the most important assets in life. It took the tragedy of cancer to remind our oldest of that valuable lesson. And at the same time, it also taught us patience and how to love people through the worst of circumstances. There were relationships we thought would never mend, because it didn't happen according to our schedule, and in our way. But as we all sat together cheering for Mason's game, God reminded us of that fun chemistry lesson that change needs a catalyst. In our husbands, wives, children, and extended families, LOVE is a CATALYST.
*"...if I have faith that can move mountains but have not love, I am nothing"*
*(1 Cor. 13:2).*

*And now these three remain: faith, hope, and love. But the greatest of these is love.*
*(1 Corinthians 13:13)*

# Notes from the Author

Thank you for allowing me to share our story. I pray that you were able to feel the range of emotions that resonated in our family as we endured this test. It was my intent to share the moments of agony as well as those of victory, painting a deeply emotional picture of how we responded. Life is complicated, and so are the situations we face. Whether your family is challenged with a devastating illness, a Prodigal child, or the trials of divorce and/or blending a family, I hope that you have been encouraged by our testimony.

I often struggled with how much to share, and have done my best to consider the feelings of all involved. To that point, while Malcolm's mom was involved in his treatment, I did not feel it my place to convey her emotions during this ordeal. I will add that we all worked together to help our boys through a very difficult and trying time.

Our whole family was impacted by Malcolm's illness. Even the youngest Hill, Matthew, had this to say: "When I first heard that my brother Malcolm had cancer, I cried. When he had cancer, every night I was so worried about him. Every time my mom would say "Okay, we are going to the hospital" I would be so excited. When he would have surgery, I would ask "So, that means he won't have cancer anymore?" but she would answer "I sure hope not". Every day I would hope that he didn't have cancer anymore. I was so relieved when they put the metal in his knee. When he rang the bell, I was the happiest person in the world!"

No matter the situation, there is always a reason, and God always has a plan to use it for your good and His glory.

**Alana M. Hill** is an energetic, globetrotting wife, mother, small business owner, and faithful servant. Born and raised in Texas, she received a bachelor's degree in Petroleum Engineering from Texas A&M University. Alana married her best friend, Rodney, and together they raised four handsome boys. Family has always been Alana's highest priority, and prompted her to establish a home-based consulting practice. A passionate youth ministry leader and teacher, she has continued to pour God's love into children she encounters, and offers encouragement to parents of children of all ages. Her faith, and desire to encourage others, led to her latest endeavor of becoming an author and speaker. Alana resides in Sugar Land, TX, where you will find her running and serving in her community. She can be contacted at info@loveisacatalyst.com

For more on Alana and how the Hill family came to be, read *Love is a Catalyst: In the Beginning.* A deeply personal memoir about coming into adulthood and how her childhood pains impacted her parenting. Learn the lessons that helped prepare her spiritually and emotionally for the journey you just witnessed.

www.ingramcontent.com/pod-product-compliance
Lightning Source LLC
LaVergne TN
LVHW051502070426
835507LV00022B/2888